A GOOD AND JOYFUL THING

A GOOD AND JOYFUL THING

THE EVOLUTION OF THE EUCHARISTIC PRAYER

BYRON D. STUHLMAN

 CHURCH

Church Publishing Incorporated, New York

Library of Congress Cataloging-in-Publication Data

Stuhlman, Byron D.
A good and joyful thing : the evolution of the Eucharistic prayer /
Byron D. Stuhlman.
       p. cm.
    Includes bibliographical references.
    ISBN 0-89869-338-1 (pbk.)
    1. Eucharistic prayers—History.
    2. Eucharistic prayers—Episcopal Church—History
    3. Eucharistic prayers—Anglican Communion—History.
    4. Episcopal Church—Liturgy—History.
    5. Anglican Communion—Liturgy—History. I. Title.
    BV825.54 .S88 2000
    264'.36—dc21   00-064394

Church Publishing Incorporated
445 Fifth Avenue
New York NY 10016

5 4 3 2 1

TABLE OF CONTENTS

❖ ❖ ❖ ❖ ❖ ❖ ❖ ❖ ❖ ❖ ❖ ❖ ❖

INTRODUCTION
THIS OUR SACRIFICE OF PRAISE AND THANKSGIVING

❖ ❖ ❖ ❖ ❖ ❖ ❖ ❖ ❖ ❖ ❖ ❖

THE SHAPE OF THE EUCHARIST AND THE SHAPE OF THE EUCHARISTIC PRAYER

Dom Gregory Dix's *Shape of the Liturgy*, first published in 1945,[1] decisively influenced the way in which we understand the eucharistic liturgy. In that work he shifted our attention from the *text* of the liturgy to the sequence of actions which constitute the liturgy. Today we are accustomed to think of the eucharist as consisting (in the words of the full title found in the 1979 Book of Common Prayer 1979) of

(1) The Proclamation of the Word of God and

(2) The Celebration of the Holy Communion.

The principal actions of the first part of the service, as outlined in An Order for Celebrating the Holy Eucharist, are (1) gathering, (2) reading and proclaiming the Word of God, (3) offering prayers of intercession, and (4) exchanging the peace. The principal actions of the second part of the service are (1) preparing the bread and wine, (2) giving thanks, (3) breaking the bread, and (4) sharing the bread and wine in communion. This structure underlies the changes made by most Christian churches in the liturgical revisions of the second half of the twentieth century and reflects a broad consensus among the churches.

But the action of giving thanks is a *verbal* action, and therefore does involve a text—the eucharistic prayer, which is the church's sacrifice of praise and thanksgiving. Although many scholars attempted to find a common structure for the eucharistic prayer during the revision of the mid-twentieth century, consensus on this issue was more apparent than real. In order to identify such a common structure, some scholars superimposed upon the classical eucharistic prayers of the pre-Reformation traditions the structure of West Syrian prayers, such as the anaphoras of St. Basil, St. James, and St. John Chrysostom. But to do so, they had to modify that structure somewhat, and the result does not respect the thematic integrity of the eucharistic prayer in the various traditions or take adequate account of how they reached their present form.[2]

More recently scholars, working from a general consensus that the eucharistic prayer developed out of the Jewish meal blessing known as the *Birkat-ha-Mazon*, have argued that the structure common to all classical eucharistic prayers is a movement from praise and thanksgiving in the first part of the eucharistic prayer to supplication in the second part. Later eucharistic prayers developed as the thanksgiving and the supplication were expanded, and new components (such as the Sanctus with its introduction and the institution narrative with its anamnesis) were added. The differing placement of the Sanctus (between two sections of thanksgiving or just before the supplication) and of the institution narrative with its anamnesis (as a component of the thanksgiving or as a component of the supplication) lies behind the structural diversity of classical eucharistic prayers. Anglican liturgists have recently declared a preference for the West Syrian pattern, with the Sanctus concluding the first thanksgiving, the institution narrative and anamnesis concluding the second thanksgiving, and an invocation of the Spirit upon the church and its offering at the beginning of the supplication.[3]

THE EUCHARISTIC PRAYER IN THE SCOTTISH-AMERICAN TRADITION

That was the pattern adopted by the Scottish Episcopal Church in the Communion Office of 1764 and by the American Episcopal Church in the Prayer Book of 1789. The American church retained the pattern for Eucharistic Prayers I, II, A, B, and D in the Prayer Book of 1979. It would seem, then, that a consistent structure for the eucharistic prayer has been maintained by the Episcopal Church and that there is no need for the Episcopal Church to rethink its eucharistic theology.

In reality that is not the case. While the structure of the eucharistic prayer has been consistent in this tradition, a review of the historical background reveals considerable shifts in the understanding of that prayer and its function over the course of the centuries (as we shall see in far more detail in chapter 5). A brief review of the history of the Anglican liturgical traditions will reveal these shifts, which are signaled by studying (1) the name and integrity of the eucharistic prayer, (2) the thematic structure of the eucharistic prayer, (3) the theology implicit in the text of the eucharistic prayer, and (4) the theological interpretation of the eucharistic prayer.

The Name and Integrity of the Eucharistic Prayer

The names "Eucharistic Prayer" and "Great Thanksgiving" were first introduced into the Prayer Book in 1979 (and the preliminary drafts for that book). Before that time, the text was treated as two or more prayers. In the West Syrian liturgical tradition the eucharistic prayer has always been treated as a single text, which is usually called the anaphora or (prayer of) "offering." In the Roman tradition, the title Canon (which we might render "prescribed form") was at first given to the entire text but later used for the text which follows the Sanctus. The initial portion of the text has been known as the Preface—a term originally understood as "solemn proclamation" and also used for the entire prayer but later understood as "proem" or "introduction." But when the Preface is not understood as an integral part of the prayer, the character of the prayer as thanksgiving is severely weakened or lost.

After the Reformation, the term Prayer of Consecration replaced the term Canon, but the Preface continued to be treated as distinct from the part of the text which follows the Sanctus—even in the Scottish-American strand of the Anglican tradition which took the West Syrian anaphoras as its model. In the English text after 1552 and in the American text until 1928, the distinction between the Preface and the Prayer of Consecration was further emphasized by the intrusion of the Prayer of Humble Access between them. The Eucharistic Prayer may legitimately be understood as a Prayer of Consecration. But the theological understanding of this prayer as a prayer of consecration is altered when the Preface is not included as an integral part of that prayer—particularly at a time when most liturgists are moving toward a consensus that we consecrate by giving thanks rather than by reciting a particular formula (whether that formula be an invocation of the Holy Spirit or the words of Christ at the last supper). The 1979 inclusion of the Preface as a part of the Great Thanksgiving therefore signals an important shift in the understanding of the Eucharistic Prayer, even when the text of that prayer remains unaltered.

The Structure of the Eucharistic Prayer

Although Cranmer paraphrased and rearranged the components of the Roman Eucharistic Prayer, he retained its basic thematic structure, which moves from thanksgiving in the Preface to supplication in the Canon. The Scottish-American tradition, beginning with the Scottish Communion Office of 1764, recast the components into the thematic structure of West Syrian anaphoras—a first thanksgiving in the Preface, a second thanksgiving beginning with the introduction to the institution narrative in the first section of the Prayer of Consecration, and a Supplication, beginning with the Invocation. In the Roman structure, the institution narrative is part of the supplication; in the West Syrian structure it is part of the second thanksgiving. In chapter 8 and the conclusion, we shall see why the precise sequence of institution narrative, anamnesis/oblation, invocation, and supplication in the West Syrian and Scottish-American structure avoids problems raised by other thematic structures.

The Theology Implicit in the Text of the Eucharistic Prayer

The Great Thanksgiving is both a prayer of consecration and a prayer of oblation. But these theological themes are worked out differently in the various texts before us. In the Roman canon, the logic of the text suggests that the consecration is effected by two petitions for the acceptance of the church's offering, the Quam oblationem before the institution narrative and the Supra quae/Supplices which follows the institution narrative and anamnesis. From the early middle ages, however, interpreters understood the consecration to be effected by the recitation by the priest, acting in persona Christi, of the words of Christ over the bread and over the cup.

Cranmer's 1549 text suggests that the consecration is effected by the invocation of the Holy Spirit and by the "word" of the institution narrative. The removal of the invocation in the English text after 1552 suggests that it is the petition for a fruitful communion which replaced the invocation that consecrates. The Scottish text after 1637 and the American text invoke both Christ and the Holy Spirit upon the bread and wine ("Word" being no longer understood as the text of the institution narrative, but as Christ the Word), suggesting that it is the invocation that consecrates (although the institution narrative was still considered an essential component of the prayer). John Johnson held that the proper sequence of components in the consecration was institution narrative, oblation, and invocation, and that all of these had a part to play in the consecration, and this is reflected in the structure of Scottish text after 1764 and the American text.

The text of the Roman canon, the English text of 1549, and the Scottish text after 1637 suggest a doctrine of the real presence of Christ associated with the consecrated elements, although all these texts except the Scottish text after 1764 by their wording might be read in a receptionist manner, since all except the Scottish text after 1764 ask that the bread and the wine might become "to us" Christ's body and blood. The English text after 1552 and the American text suggest a receptionist doctrine with their petition that communicants might be partakers of Christ's body and blood, although these texts do not exclude a presence associated with the elements.

The doctrine of eucharistic sacrifice is a more complex issue. The text of the Roman canon suggests that the bread and wine are offered by the church both as elements of creation and as figures of Christ's sacrificial offering. But when the words of Christ in the institution narrative are understood as consecratory, then the subsequent oblation of the elements might suggest that what the church is offering in the eucharist is Christ himself—a doctrine which caused the Reformers to avoid any identification of the bread and wine with the church's offering. Cranmer's 1549 text suggests that the eucharist is celebrated as a "perpetual memory" of Christ's "one sacrifice of himself once offered" and that the church's "sacrifice of praise and thanksgiving" is the communicants' self-oblation. The Prayer of Oblation which follows the institution narrative in the 1549 English text and the 1637 Scottish text is not an oblation of the elements, but an oblation of the communicants. In English Prayer Books after 1552 this prayer is reworked and used as an alternative postcommunion prayer.

The Scottish text since 1764 and the American text recast the oblation as an offering of "these thy holy gifts which we now offer unto thee" as well as an oblation of "ourselves, our souls and bodies, to be a reasonable, holy, and living sacrifice." Moreover, the elements offered in the eucharistic prayer have already been rubrically offered when they are prepared during the offertory in the Scottish and American tradition—a preliminary oblation which was intentionally eliminated in the 1979 Prayer Book.

The Theological Interpretation of the Eucharistic Prayer

The theology implicit in texts is not always the theology read into texts. We have already seen that this is the case with the doctrines of consecration and of eucharistic sacrifice in terms of the Roman canon. The same is true of Anglican texts. There have been Scottish and American Anglicans who held a doctrine of consecration by the words of Christ, even though such a doctrine is difficult to reconcile with the text of the eucharistic prayer in these two traditions. This is ritually indicated whenever the bread and wine are elevated *after* the words "This is my body" and "This is my blood" and reverence is paid to the elements at this point. Such elevations have never been prescribed by the rubrics, and were forbidden by Cranmer in 1549, but there have been periods when they were common.

In terms of the doctrine of eucharistic presence, the theology of the Scottish texts suggest an association of that presence with the elements, while the theology of the American texts suggests a receptionist doctrine which associates the presence with the communicants. Nevertheless, the American church since the time of the Oxford movement has generally held to a doctrine of the real presence which is less receptionist than the text of its eucharistic prayer would suggest. This consensus is reflected in the new eucharistic prayers found in the 1979 Prayer Book.

As regards the doctrine of eucharistic sacrifice, the broad consensus in both Scottish and American churches favors the doctrine suggested by the text of their eucharistic prayers. But there have been many who have held to a doctrine of eucharistic sacrifice which is much closer to medieval Catholic doctrine, understanding it in some sense as an offering of Christ.

An adequate understanding of all of these issues requires us to undertake a study of the evolution of the eucharistic prayer, not just in Anglicanism, but in the history of the Christian church.

An Overview of this Study

What becomes clear as we trace the development of the eucharistic prayer is that there is no single line of development for eucharistic prayers. In the following chapters we will look at how early eucharistic prayers developed out of Jewish meal blessings, how different traditions expanded these prayers, incorporating such material as the Sanctus, and the account of the institution of the eucharist, how the reformers understood the eucharist and shaped their rites accordingly, and what the results of twentieth-century liturgical reforms have been. A concomitant feature of these developments has been a series of shifts in how the church understands the eucharistic prayer to function—shifts which are conventionally treated as the theology of consecration and the theology of the eucharistic sacrifice. We will take note as we follow the development of the eucharistic prayer of how these shifts in the understanding of its function interacted with developments in the text of the prayer itself. The student of the eucharistic prayer now has most of the relevant texts readily available in R. C. D. Jasper and G. J. Cuming, *Prayers of the Eucharist: Early and Reformed* (third edition, Collegeville, Minn.: Liturgical Press, 1990). The task of this present work is to tease out of these texts the lines of development and the theology which lay behind that development.

The following summary of subsequent chapters will give the reader a map of how this investigation will unfold:

> **Chapter 1** examines the customary blessings for a Jewish festal meal and the way in which those blessings are transformed by reference to Christ in the earliest eucharistic texts to come down to us—the prayers found in chapters 9 and 10 of the church manual known to us as the *Didache*. It concludes with a look at how the table blessings of this rite would evolve into a single eucharistic prayer in the coming centuries.
>
> **Chapter 2** looks at how the eucharistic prayers described in the baptismal homilies of Cyril of Jerusalem and Theodore of Mopsuestia interpreted the church's worship as a sacrament of participation in the heavenly liturgy and so incorporated the angelic hymn (the Sanctus) as a central feature of the eucharistic

prayer. Then the anaphora of St. James is analyzed to see if we can find embedded in it a eucharistic prayer which conforms to the prayer described by Cyril.

Chapter 3 looks at the development of the standard West Syrian structure for the eucharistic prayer, analyzing the prayer found in the *Apostolic Tradition*, the anaphoras ascribed to Basil of Caesarea and John Chrysostom, and the final form of the anaphora of St. James.

Chapter 4 looks at the parallel structures behind the texts of what we know as the Alexandrian anaphora of St. Mark and the Roman canon and then reviews the structure of the eucharistic prayers of the Gallican and Mozarabic traditions.

A Review looks back on the evolution of the structure and theology of the eucharistic prayer from the initial nucleus of thanksgiving and supplication in the Christian version of Jewish table blessings to the classic eucharistic prayers of the fourth and fifth centuries.

Chapter 5 looks at the eucharistic rites of the Lutheran tradition, where the proclamation of the eucharistic gospel rather than giving thanks is understood to fulfill the function of consecrating the elements.

Chapter 6 examines how the Reformed tradition understands the eucharistic action and the prayers which grow out of that understanding.

Chapter 7 examines the two strands of development in the eucharistic prayers of the Anglican tradition—the English tradition growing out of the Prayer Book of 1552 and the Scottish-American tradition growing out of the reshaping of the 1549 Prayer Book in the Scottish Prayer Book of 1637 and the Scottish Communion Office of 1764.

Chapter 8 explores the eucharistic prayers that have grown out of a renewed understanding of the eucharist in the twentieth century and the issues that have arisen in crafting these prayers.

The Conclusion will explore the issues which the Episcopal Church will need to address as it undertakes the next revision of the Book of Common Prayer in the light of the eucharistic theology articulated in the work of the International Anglican Liturgical Consultation. These issues include the rubrical requirement for manual acts during the institution narrative and the placement of the memorial acclamation in the structure of the eucharistic prayer. Eucharistic Prayer 3 in *Enriching Our Worship* signals a shift on both of these issues which is noteworthy.

NOTES

[1] Gregory Dix, *The Shape of the Liturgy* (London: A & C Black, 1945; New York: Seabury Press, 1982).

[2] The most notable attempt to outline such a structure was made by W. Jardine Grisbrooke. See the discussion below in the Conclusion.

[3] See the recommendations in *Our Thanks and Praise: The Eucharist in Anglicanism Today. Papers from the Fifth International Anglican Liturgical Consultation.* Toronto: Anglican Book Centre, 1998.

CHAPTER ONE

FROM JEWISH BLESSINGS TO THE CHRISTIAN EUCHARISTIC PRAYER

❖ ❖ ❖ ❖ ❖ ❖ ❖ ❖ ❖ ❖ ❖ ❖ ❖

THE *BERAKOTH* USED AT THE LAST SUPPER

On the evening that he was betrayed, Jesus shared his final meal with his disciples. It remains a matter of unresolved dispute whether that meal was a passover seder or not, but in either case Jesus no doubt used the customary Jewish blessings (*berakoth*) as he presided at the supper. Two blessings figure in the biblical accounts of that supper given by Mark, Matthew, and Paul, who tell us that Jesus "blessed" the bread and "gave thanks" over the cup. Paul and Luke vary the wording slightly, reporting that Jesus "gave thanks" over the bread. Luke (in the longer version of his text) gives a fuller account: he reports that Jesus gave thanks over a cup, then over the bread, and after supper over a final cup. As he distributed the bread and the cup he said, "This is my body" and "This is my blood of the covenant."[1] And he commanded his followers to do this in remembrance of him.

Dom Gregory Dix, following the position taken by many Anglican scholars in the first half of the twentieth century, forcefully argued in the *Shape of the Liturgy* that the prayers which Jesus would have used for the bread and the cup at the last supper were the *berakoth* which have come down to us in Jewish tradition for this purpose. Subsequent scholars have generally concurred, although—as we shall see—they have nuanced his claim somewhat. Jewish tradition knows two types of *berakoth*: first, short *berakoth* such as those recited over wine and bread at a meal, and, second, longer *berakoth* such as the one recited at the end of a meal. The texts for the blessings of the wine and the bread are as follows:

> **Over the Cup of Wine:**
> Blessed art thou, O Lord our God, King of the universe,
> who createst the fruit of the vine.
>
> **Over the Bread**
> Blessed art thou, O Lord our God, King of the universe,
> who bringest forth bread from the earth.[2]

The text of the blessing at the end of the meal, known as the *Birkat ha-Mazon*, is a longer text consisting of three strophes (a final strophe was added later). The initial strophe begins in the form customary with the short *berakoth* (Blessed art thou...). The second strophe takes another common prayer form in Judaism, beginning, "We give thanks to thee..." The final strophe is a petition or supplication. But each is concluded with a final short *berakah* as a "seal" or, as we might term it, a doxology. This is a translation of the text of the three strophes as found in the earliest manuscript:

> Blessed art thou, O Lord our God, King of the universe, who feedest us and the whole world with goodness, kindness, and mercy. Blessed art thou, who dost nourish all.
>
> We give thanks to thee, O Lord our God, because thou hast given us for our inheritance a desirable land, good and wide, the covenant and the law, life and food. And for all these things we give thee thanks and bless thy name for ever and ever. Blessed art thou, O Lord, for the land and for the food.
>
> Have mercy, O Lord our God, on us thy people and on thy city Jerusalem, on thy sanctuary and thy dwelling-place, on Zion, the habitation of thy glory, and on the great and holy house over which thy Name is invoked. Restore the kingdom of the house of David to its place in our days, and speedily build Jerusalem. Blessed art thou, Lord, who buildest Jerusalem.[3]

Of this final series of *berakoth*, Dix has this to say:

> The petitions of the last paragraph must have been recast...after the destruction of the Temple in A. D. 70. But all Jewish scholars seem to be agreed that at least the first two paragraphs in substantially their present form were in use in Palestine in our Lord's time.[4]

These *berakoth* were prescribed for any meal. The final *Birkat ha-Mazon* was customarily said over a cup of wine, which would first have been blessed with the standard blessing. If the last supper was a passover meal, the blessing over a cup of wine at the beginning would have been coupled with a blessing to sanctify the feast (the *Kiddush*). The blessing of the bread would likewise have been coupled at the last supper with a blessing of unleavened bread if this were a passover meal. Finally, rabbinic prescriptions prescribe an opening dialogue for the *Birkat ha-Mazon*, which varies according to the number present for the meal.[5]

Various scholars have nuanced Dix's claims somewhat, as we shall see later. As Dix himself admits, at the time of Jesus the *berakoth* were passed down in oral tradition, and the wording might vary somewhat, following a fixed thematic outline. It has been argued that in the longer *berakoth* the final seal or doxology was later than the body of the text. We also need to remember that before the emergence of rabbinic Judaism (the heir of the Pharisaic Judaism of Jesus' time) after the destruction of the temple, there were various parties of Judaism (such as the Essenes) whose euchological tradition may have had variant texts for meal blessings. It remains likely, however, that the present tradition, first codified in written form about 200 C.E., preserves texts quite close to those that Jesus would have used at the last supper and to those that his followers would have used for the sacramental meal that they celebrated in remembrance of him.

FROM FULL MEAL TO SACRAMENTAL MEAL: THE WITNESS OF THE NEW TESTAMENT

The New Testament accounts of the last supper are all to some extent shaped by the liturgical usage of the early church: they report only those details of the supper itself that would be replicated in the meal which the church came to know as the Lord's Supper. A shift is already apparent in Paul's correspondence with the Corinthians: unseemly behavior at the Lord's Supper led Paul to instruct the congregation to take their ordinary meals at home, so that the church's sacramental meal would involve only that food and drink to which Jesus gave special significance—the bread and the wine. The other foods taken between the blessing of the bread at the beginning of the meal and the thanksgiving over the cup of blessing at the end of the meal were no longer part of the rite. That is why the accounts of the last supper in Matthew and Mark no longer report that the thanksgiving over the cup came "after supper"—a detail still found in the accounts of Paul and Luke.

Other differences in the accounts also merit our attention. Luke reports a thanksgiving over an initial cup of wine. This obviously represents the *Kiddush*, the customary sanctification of the feast at the beginning of the passover meal. The rite was also observed on the sabbath, and it is possible that the first Christians adapted it to a meal on the Lord's Day. Matthew and Mark distinguish between the *blessing* over the bread at the last supper and the *thanksgiving* over the cup at the end of the meal. This may reflect a terminological distinction between the short *berakah* customary for the bread and the extended *berakah* (or series of *berakoth*) at the end of a meal. We may remember that the second strophe of the *Birkat ha-Mazon* begins, "We give thanks to thee" rather than "Blessed art thou."

THE EUCHARISTIC BLESSINGS OF THE *DIDACHE*

The Didache first came to public attention when it was discovered by Philotheos Bryennios, Greek Metropolitan of Nicomedia, in the library of the Monastery of the Holy Sepulcher in Constantinople in 1875 and was published in 1883. It had the impact of a bombshell on the customary account of the history of Christian worship. This is the earliest of a genre of early Christian literature known as church orders. It begins with catechetical material (the "two ways") and also contains directions for fasting, daily prayer, the administration of baptism, the eucharist, and regulations on local ministers (bishops and deacons), itinerant ministers (apostles and prophets) and disciplinary matters. It is a compilation of material from various sources and represents a form of early Jewish Christianity. It is now generally dated at about 100. Syria is most frequently suggested as its place of origin.

The material related to the eucharist is found in chapters 9 and 10. What we find is a thanksgiving over the cup (a single strophe) and a thanksgiving over bread (two strophes) in chapter 9 and a thanksgiving (three strophes) after partaking in chapter 10. Further directions are given in chapter 14. The material in chapters 9 and 10 is so different from later eucharistic rites that scholars have been perplexed as to what to make of it: even Gregory Dix was disposed to treat it as a fellowship meal (agape) rather than a Christian eucharist, despite the opening heading of these chapters, "About the Eucharist."

This is the text of the prayers and their introductory rubrics in these chapters:

About the Eucharist: Give thanks thus: First, about the cup:

We give thanks to thee, our Father, for the holy vine of thy servant [or "child," *pais*] David, which thou hast revealed through thy servant [*pais*] Jesus. Glory to thee for evermore.

And about the broken bread:

We give thanks to thee, our Father, for the life and knowledge which thou hast made known to us through thy servant [*pais*] Jesus Glory to thee for evermore.

As this broken bread was scattered over the mountains, and when brought together became one, so let thy Church be brought together from the ends of the earth into thy kingdom. For thine is the glory and the power through Jesus Christ for evermore.

But let no one eat or drink of your eucharist but those who have been baptized in the name of the Lord. For about this also the Lord has said, "Do not give what is holy to dogs."

After you have had your fill, give thanks thus:

We give thanks to thee, holy Father, for thy holy Name which thou hast enshrined in our hearts, and for the knowledge and faith and immortality which thou hast made known through thy servant [*pais*] Jesus. Glory to thee for evermore.

Almighty Master, thou didst create all things for the sake of thy Name, and didst give food and drink to humankind for their enjoyment, that they might give thee thanks. But to us thou hast granted spiritual food and drink and eternal life through thy servant [*pais*] Jesus. Above all we give thee thanks because thou art mighty. Glory to thee for evermore.

Remember, Lord, thy Church, to deliver it from all evil and to perfect it in thy love. Bring it together from the four winds, now sanctified, into thy kingdom which thou hast prepared for it. For thine is the power and the glory forever.

May grace come and may this world pass away.

Hosanna to the God of David.

If any is holy let him come; if any is not, let him repent. Marana tha. Amen.[6]

The prayers given in these chapters mesh closely with the description of the last supper in Luke: a thanksgiving for a first cup, one for the bread, and a thanksgiving at the end of the meal (no longer associated with a cup in the *Didache*). Note that these prayers take the form of thanksgivings rather than the blessing of God that became standard in rabbinic tradition. But it was several other features that astonished most scholars:

1. The thanksgiving over the cup precedes that over the bread (unlike the accounts of the last supper in Matthew, Mark, and Corinthians).
2. The texts make no reference to the death or resurrection of Christ.
3. The bread and wine are not described as the body and blood of Christ.

Yet if we examine closely the accounts of the last supper, the provisions of the *Didache* are what we would expect if the church followed Jesus' command to do this in remembrance of him: they give a set of blessings for the meal, Jewish in character and transformed by their reference to Christ. The blessings over the bread and the wine are Jewish in their phraseology but bear no obvious resemblance in form to the short *berakoth* prescribed in Jewish tradition. Neither begins with the standard opening for such *berakoth*, "Blessed art thou." Instead, they open with the verb found in the second strophe of the *Birkat ha-Mazon,* "we give thanks to thee." They more closely resemble the longer *berakoth* which begin in this way and conclude with a short doxology or seal, although here the doxology takes the form of "Glory to thee." The blessing over the bread also has a second strophe, a petition, unlike the Jewish *Birkat ha-Motzi.* The rubrication of the text does not tell us whether the cup and the bread are distributed separately, each after its blessing, or together at the end of the two blessings. Nor are we told what words, if any, were used during their distribution. The biblical institution narratives might lead us to expect that the formulas found in later liturgical tradition— "The body of Christ" and "The blood of Christ"—were used to administer them. It was, after all, as he distributed the elements that Jesus identified them with himself according to these accounts. But the text of the *Didache* gives no information about this.

The blessing at the end of the meal, the "postcommunion prayer," as we would call it, more closely resembles the prayer after a meal in the Jewish tradition, the *Birkat ha-Mazon.* It is introduced by a rubric that specifies its recitation "after you have had your fill." This echoes the text of Deuteronomy 8:10, "You shall eat your fill and bless the Lord your God for the good land that he has given you." This is the verse that serves as the warrant or institution for the *Birkat ha-Mazon:* some forms of that prayer include this verse in the second strophe, and the text of that strophe given above echoes its wording. Like the *Birkat ha-Mazon,* the prayer in chapter 10 of the *Didache* consists of three strophes—in this case two thanksgivings and a supplication. There are differences as well as similarities, however. The first strophe of the Christian text resembles the second strophe of the Jewish one. Each of these two strophes is thematically a thanksgiving for God's work of redemption and revelation. The final strophe of both Jewish and Christian prayers is a supplication. The Jewish supplication is for the building of Jerusalem and the restoration of the Davidic kingdom. The Christian supplication is transformed into a petition for the gathering of the church and the establishment of the messianic kingdom. The first strophe of the Jewish prayer has parallels with the second strophe of the Christian text. Here, however, the thanksgiving is not just for the food which God provides to all, but also for the *spiritual* food and drink which God has given us (the baptized).

The significance which Christians gave to the bread and wine in this sacramental meal no doubt led to fuller blessings over these elements than was customary at a Jewish meal. A preference for beginning the blessings with thanksgiving rather than an initial blessing of God also is noteworthy. A desire to conform the prayers before receiving the elements to the fuller prayer after receiving them may also have led to the additional strophe in the thanksgiving over the bread, resulting in a total of three strophes in the prayers over the elements parallel to the three strophes of the postcommunion thanksgiving.

We have seen why, from the perspective of the accounts of the last supper, there is no reason to expect the prayer to identify the bread and wine as Christ's body and blood. There is also no compelling reason to expect the prayer to include the account of the institution. The biblical account is a warrant for the Christian celebration, not the text of its prayer. Paul's account of the last supper in 1 Corinthians (11:26) has led us to understand it as the means of proclaiming Christ's death. But this represents Paul's interpretation of the rite—an interpretation which will not necessarily be taken up into the prayers associated with the rite in every Christian tradition.

We should note, finally, the early tradition of freedom in the formulation of prayers for the eucharist. The compiler of the *Didache* presents a set of prayers, but at the end of chapter 10 he advises, "In the case of prophets, however, you should let them give thanks in their own way."

FORM-CRITICAL ANALYSIS OF JEWISH AND CHRISTIAN TEXTS

In recent decades scholars have paid close attention to the varying forms that prayer may take in the Jewish tradition.[7] We have noted that some accounts of the supper describe the prayer over the bread as a "blessing" (eulogia) and the prayer over the cup (the *Birkat ha-Mazon*) as a "thanksgiving" (eucharistia). Until the last few decades of the twentieth century, many scholars treated the two words as equivalent, carefully analyzed the standard Jewish form of the *berakah*, and treated the Christian *eucharistia* from their analysis of the Jewish *berakah*. The most important of the studies which worked from this perspective was that of Jean-Paul Audet, who distinguished in Jewish prayer forms two categories of *berakoth*: short spontaneous *berakoth* (such as those over the cup and the bread) which opened by blessing God ("Blessed art thou, O Lord our God, King of the worlds") and concluded with the motive for the blessing ("who bringest forth bread from the earth") and longer "cultic" *berakoth*. He analyzed this second form as consisting of an opening benediction, a second part which he characterizes as an anamnesis of the *mirabilia Dei* (an expansion of the motive in shorter blessings); and a concluding benediction as a doxology.[8]

While *berakah* was the name which Jewish tradition gave to its standard prayers, it has proved misleading to treat all forms with this name as a single genre. Later scholars have criticized Audet for equating eulogia and eucharistia in this way. Joseph Heinemann's *Prayer in the Talmud: Forms and Patterns* (Berlin/New York, 1977) was a ground-breaking work in critical examination of Jewish prayer forms. While not all of Heinemann's conclusions have gone without challenge,[9] his study has forced Christian scholars to bring a more nuanced approach to their analysis of the way in which the Jewish *berakoth* were taken over into Christian worship. Robert Ledogar[10] and Thomas Talley[11] in particular have criticized Audet's analysis of the longer or "cultic" *berakoth*. They note that the tradition knows three forms of these *berakoth*: the form which begins "Blessed art thou," like the shorter *berakoth*; the forms that begin "we confess" or "we give thanks" (as this verb—*ydh*—is often rendered in translation); and forms that begin with a straightforward narrative or statement in either the second or the third person. There are also, of course, intercessory forms which begin with a petition. It is the final seal with which these prayers conclude that conforms them to the genre of *berakoth*. The eucharistic prayers of the Christian church favored, as we have seen, the opening "we give thanks": all of the blessings of the *Didache* except the supplications begin in this way, as do most later eucharistic prayers. With this background, we might contrast the structure of the three strophes of *Birkat ha-Mazon* with the structure of the three strophes of chapter 10 of the *Didache* (and the parallel structure of the three strophes of chapter 9) as follows:

Birkat ha-Mazon	*Didache*
Blessing with blessing as a seal	Thanksgiving with doxology
Thanksgiving with blessing as a seal	Thanksgiving with doxology
Supplication with blessing as a seal	Supplication with expanded doxology

Two recent scholars have paid particular attention to a feature of the Jewish *berakoth* (particularly the *Birkat ha-Mazon*) which they believe has a bearing on Christian eucharistic prayers—though it does not arise in reference to the blessings of the *Didache*. The *Birkat ha-Mazon* is modified by the incorporation of additional texts (generally referred to as embolisms) on certain feasts. On Hanukkah and Purim the embolism is added to the second strophe. On Passover it is added to the third strophe. Louis Ligier was interested in how the institution narrative came to be incorporated in the eucharistic prayer.[12] He understood this narrative and the anamnesis which is coupled with it as a Christian equivalent of the festal embolism in the *Birkat ha-Mazon*.

Cesare Giraudo also deals with this issue,[13] but he treats it in connection with his own analysis of the origins of Christian eucharistic prayers. He argues that the dominant model for the Christian eucharistic prayer was not the Jewish *berakoth*, but rather the form that prayers of confession take in the Old Testament. The confession can either be a confession of thanks for what God has done or a confession of sin on the part of God's people. For purposes of comparison to Christian eucharistic prayers the confession of thanks represents the key use of this form of prayer. Giraudo contrasts this form (which he calls *todah*) with the rabbinic *berakah*. The texts start out with a confession of God's mighty deeds in narrative form and go on to ask God to act in the present on the basis of the past deeds just acknowledged in the confession. Giraudo speaks of the two parts of such texts somewhat anachronistically as anamnetic and epicletic. On this basis he treats Christian eucharistic texts as bipartite (thanksgiving/supplication) rather than tripartite (blessing or thanksgiving/thanksgiving/supplication).

Giraudo, like Ligier, speaks of embolisms in the text of Jewish and Christian prayers. But Giraudo uses the term somewhat differently from Ligier. His reference is to texts incorporated into the prayers which cite the institution of a rite. This is not the function of the festal embolisms of the *Birkat ha-Mazon*. The kind of embolism of which Giraudo speaks is to be found rather in the allusion to or direct citation of Deuteronomy 8:10 in the second strophe of various forms of this prayer. That citation is in fact much closer to the way in which later eucharistic prayers would incorporate the account of the institution of the Lord's Supper. That, however, is a much longer text, is seldom cited in the actual words of any one account of the institution in the New Testament, and is usually followed by the anamnesis, a non-biblical text. A closer parallel to the Jewish citation of Deuteronomy 8:10 is actually found in Christian use of Malachi 1:11: "For from the rising of the sun to its setting my name is great among the nations, and in every place incense is offered to my name, and a pure offering, for my name is great among the nations, says the Lord of hosts." Enrico Mazza pays particular attention to the use of this text in his study, *The Origins of the Eucharistic Prayer*. The text from Malachi is cited by the *Didache*—not in the blessings themselves, but in the regulations found in chapter 14. We do find this citation incorporated into the actual text of a eucharistic prayer in the Alexandrian anaphora of St. Mark. There it occurs, as we shall see later, in the second strophe of the prayer, both in the short form of the text in the Strasbourg Papyrus and in the expanded text of the later rite.

THE FORMATION OF EUCHARISTIC PRAYERS FROM THE TABLE BLESSINGS

At least three factors were at work in the formation of the later eucharistic prayers from *berakoth* or table blessings of the Jewish tradition:

1. The shift from a full meal to a sacramental meal involving only the elements to which Jesus gave special significance at the last supper meant that the significant blessings followed one another in close succession. Already in the *Didache* it is possible that the cup and the bread were both blessed before either was distributed to the participants. A document as late as the *Didascalia* (probably early

third century) speaks (2:58) of allowing a visiting bishop to pronounce the blessing over the cup in the eucharistic rite.

2. While the most important meal blessing in the Jewish tradition was the blessing at the end of the meal, the significance attributed to the bread and wine by Jesus at the last supper gave increased importance to the blessings recited before partaking of these elements and led to fuller blessings at this point—as we see again in the *Didache*, where the blessings of the cup and the bread in chapter 9 are equal in length to the blessing in chapter 10 after partaking of these elements.

3. While the rhetorical conventions of Semitic prayer favored a eucharistic prayer composed of a series of discrete *berakoth*, the rhetorical conventions of Greek prayer favored a single, logically ordered eucharistic prayer. Semitic conventions continued to prevail in the Syriac eucharistic prayers of the East Syrian tradition, composed of a series of *gehantas*;[14] but in the West Syrian tradition, rhetorical conventions led to the carefully structured Greek anaphoras familiar to us in the prayers attributed to Basil, John Chrysostom, and James.

LOOKING TOWARD THE FUTURE

By the mid-second century, a service of readings and intercessions (the liturgy of the word) had been joined to the church's sacramental meal to form the service for the Lord's Day which we find outlined in chapters 65 and 67 of the *First Apology* of Justin Martyr. We have no documentation of how this development took place, but it seems likely that as Christians were expelled from the synagogue they joined a liturgy which resembled the sabbath service of the synagogue to the sacramental meal of the Lord's Day. This development may have occurred at about the same time as the table blessings were fused into a single eucharistic prayer. Justin Martyr gives a general description of such a prayer: the presiding minister "sends up prayers and thanksgivings to the best of his ability, and the people assent, saying the Amen."[15] From this general description we can gather little except that the thanksgivings and supplications were said over the bread and wine and that the celebrant enjoyed a certain degree of liberty in formulating such a prayer.

Since the eucharist was understood as the anamnesis of Christ, later prayers moved toward a much expanded narrative of the economy of salvation in Christ somewhere in the course of the prayer. Three further components found their way into later prayers. The first of these is the Sanctus, with its introduction and sometimes with appended material (the first epiclesis of the Alexandrian tradition). The second is the institution narrative as a warrant for the celebration. The anamnesis (which articulates the church's intention to "do this" in remembrance of Christ) is usually appended to this narrative. These two components entered the eucharistic prayers of the various traditions at different times and at different points in the structure of the prayer. A final component is the expansion of the supplication. There are two aspects to the expansion of this part of the text. First, the supplication for the communicants (or the church) frequently developed into an invocation of the Spirit upon the communicants and their offerings (especially in the West Syrian tradition) or an extended prayer for the acceptance of the church's offering (in the Roman tradition). Second, the scope of the intercession in the supplication was generally greatly expanded.

We should also note that as the church lost its original close contact with Judaism, the shape of the eucharistic prayer was less directly influenced by the standard Jewish meal blessings. While the nucleus of some later eucharistic prayers seems to resemble the tripartite shape of the *Birkat ha-Mazon* (two thanksgivings and a supplication) in general the most striking feature is the movement of the prayer from thanksgiving to supplication—a feature which seems to be the enduring heritage of the Jewish roots of the prayer.

THE THEOLOGY OF THE EUCHARIST IN THE *DIDACHE*

The theology of the blessings of the *Didache* is rooted, as we might expect, in the theology of blessing in the Jewish tradition. As Louis Bouyer notes,[16] the New Testament gives succinct expression to this theology in 1 Timothy 4:4 :

> ...everything created by God is good, and nothing is to be rejected, provided it is received with thanksgiving; for it is sanctified by God's word and by prayer.

The idea here is that created things are restored to God's purposes for them when God is blessed for them and we acknowledge God's purposes, usually by citing the scriptural text (God's word) which sets out that purpose. This is a good description of the *berakoth*, which consist of a blessing of God and a citation of the motive or warrant for blessing him. Deuteronomy 8:10 is thus incorporated by allusion or citation into various versions of the *Birkat ha-Mazon* as a warrant. For early Christians as for Jews, the Old Testament was the "scripture" where they might seek such warrant: early authors cite Malachi 1:11 as the warrant for the eucharist. In the *Didache* it is found in the rubrics rather than the text of the blessings, but—as we shall see—the citation was incorporated into the text of some later prayers. Once the New Testament became "scripture" for Christians, it could provide the warrant for the celebration of the eucharist. Christ's command to do this as his anamnesis ("in remembrance of me") in many of the accounts of the last supper or an allusion to 1 Corinthians 11:26 might function in this way.

If the church follows Christ's command, it "gives thanks" to God for the bread and wine of its sacramental meal and by so doing celebrates Christ's anamnesis and proclaims his death. In other words, the bread and wine are consecrated for their sacramental purpose by giving thanks over them. Jesus identified the bread and wine as his body and blood as he distributed them to his disciples. We might expect Christian celebrations to make the identification in the same way—in the words of administration. Consequently, the identification need not necessarily be made in the text of the blessing or eucharistic prayer, although later Christians would feel the need to do so.

We have already noted early references to Malachi 1:11 as the warrant for the Christian eucharist. Early apologetic literature made significant use of this text. It was important for Christians in two ways. Sacrifice was the primary form of cult in late antiquity, and Christians were sometimes accused of atheism because they had no sacrificial priesthood, no sacrifice, and no temple as a place of sacrifice. The Christian response was that their form of sacrifice was a sacrifice of praise and thanksgiving in the form of prayer. This approach is already to be found in 1 Peter in the New Testament, where the whole church is understood as a "royal priesthood" called to "proclaim the mighty acts of the one who called you out of darkness into his marvelous light" and to "offer spiritual sacrifices acceptable to God through Jesus Christ."[17] While sacrifice was important to many in late antiquity, the Christian claim had appeal to growing numbers of people for whom animal sacrifice no longer seemed an appropriate form for the worship of God.

The early emphasis was on the prayer of praise and thanksgiving as the form of sacrifice. But as Christians encountered the gnostic denial of the goodness of material creation, they began to associate their sacrifice of praise and thanksgiving with the offering of the bread and wine used in the eucharist and to understand it as the offering of the "first-fruits" of creation[18]—still repudiating animal sacrifice, but nevertheless giving their offering material form. By the second century Christian apologists would argue that the use of bread and wine at the eucharist demonstrated the goodness of creation. The theme of sacrifice would develop in coming centuries as the eucharist as the anamnesis of Christ's death came to be understood as the memorial of his sacrifice, but we find few hints of this in the earliest literature, and it figures even in later times more in commentaries on the eucharist (such as that given by Cyril of Jerusalem in his baptismal homilies) than in the text of the eucharistic prayer.

With this background, we will turn in the following chapters to see how new blocks of material with their own distinctive themes were incorporated into the eucharistic prayers of developing local traditions—the Sanctus and related materials, an extended narrative of the economy of salvation (in the East) or a seasonally varied narrative of an aspect of that economy (in the West), the institution narrative as a warrant and the anamnesis as the pledge to fulfill that warrant, and an invocation of the Spirit (epiclesis) as a part of the supplication. As these materials were incorporated into the eucharistic prayer, structural diversity gave way to increasing uniformity by the late fourth and early fifth centuries as the major liturgical traditions emerged.

NOTES

[1] The texts in Luke and Paul read "the new covenant in my blood."

[2] My translation of the standard texts.

[3] Text from Jasper and Cuming, *Prayers of the Eucharist*, pages 10-11. (Collegeville: Liturgical Press, 3rd edition, 1990). I have recast the text somewhat to stay closer to the Hebrew idiom (in particular in the use of the second person singular). The embolisms (additions inserted in the text) are omitted, as is the final strophe, which is later. Note that the relative clauses of the *Birkat ha-Mazon* use the third person singular, although this translation and most others smooth out the text by using the second person.

[4] Gregory Dix, *The Shape of the Liturgy* (New York: Seabury Press, 1982), pages 53-54.

[5] The form that the dialogue would take is set in later rabbinic rules. We do not know what form it might have taken in the first century. In any case, the text of the dialogue that became standard in the Christian tradition does not appear to derive from the practice to which rabbinic sources give witness.

[6] Text from Jasper and Cuming, *Prayers of the Eucharist*, pages 23-24. I have recast the translation somewhat to be closer to the Greek (especially in the use of the second person singular).

[7] For good surveys of the material in this section, see Thomas J. Talley, "Sources and Structure of the Eucharistic Prayer," in his *Worship: Reforming Tradition* (Washington, D.C.: Pastoral Press, 1990); Enrico Mazza, *The Origins of the Eucharistic Prayer* (Collegeville: Liturgical Press, 1995), especially the introduction and chapter 1; and Paul R. Bradshaw, *The Search for the Origins of Christian Worship: Studies and Methods for the Study of Early Liturgy* (New York: Oxford, 1992), chapters 1 and 6.

[8] Jean-Paul Audet, "Literary Forms and Contents of a Normal Eucharistia in the first Century," *Studia Evangelica 1* (1959), pages 643-662.

[9] See the critique by Tzvee Zahany in "The Politics of Piety: Social Conflict and the Emergence of Rabbinic Liturgy," in Paul F. Bradshaw and Lawrence Hoffman, eds., *The Making of Jewish and Christian Worship* (Notre Dame: University of Notre Dame Press, 1991), pages 42-68.

[10] See *Acknowledgement: Praise Verbs in the Early Greek Anaphoras* (Rome, 1968).

[11] See Talley, "Sources and Structure of the Eucharistic Prayer," in his *Worship: Reforming Tradition* (Washington, D.C.: Pastoral Press, 1990).

[12] Louis Ligier, "From the Last Supper to the Eucharist," in L. C. Sheppard, ed., *The New Liturgy* (London, 1970), pages 113-150, and "The Origins of the Eucharistic Prayer," in *Studia Liturgica 9* (1973), pages 161-185.

[13] *La struttura letteraria della preghiera eucaristica: Saggia sulla genesi letteraria di una forma*, Analecta Biblica, vol. 92 (Rome: Biblical Institute Press, 1981).

[14] See the anaphora of Saints Addai and Mari and the third anaphora of St. Peter in Jasper and Cuming, *Prayers of the Eucharist.* The two anaphoras appear to derive from a common original. In its present form Addai and Mari lacks the institution narrative. The texts given in this edition do not note the division into gehantas, which may be found in the edition of Addai and Mari in F. E. Brightman, *Liturgies Eastern and Western* (Oxford: Clarendon Press, 1896). The East Syrian liturgy was reformed by the patriarch Iso 'Yabh II in the seventh century, and there is no scholarly consensus about the form that the texts took before that date.

[15] *First Apology,* chapter 67. Translation from Jaspers and Cuming, *Prayers of the Eucharist*, page 30.

[16] Louis Bouyer, *Liturgical Piety* (Notre Dame: University of Notre Dame Press, 1955), page 119.

[17] 1 Peter 2:9, 4-5.

[18] See Justin Martyr, *Dialogue with Trypho the Jew*, chapter 41; and Irenaeus, *Against all Heresies*, 4:17.5.

CHAPTER TWO

A SACRAMENT OF THE HEAVENLY LITURGY
CYRIL OF JERUSALEM, THEODORE OF MOPSUESTIA, AND THE ANAPHORA OF ST. JAMES

❖ ❖ ❖ ❖ ❖ ❖ ❖ ❖ ❖ ❖ ❖ ❖

INTRODUCTION: THE BIBLICAL BASIS

In the Book of Exodus, the temple which Israel is commanded to build is to be based on a heavenly archetype or pattern. When God appeared to Moses in the cloud on Mt. Sinai, he commanded him:

> According to all that I show you concerning the pattern of the tabernacle, and of all its furniture, so shall you make it.... See that you make them according to the pattern for them, which is being shown to you on the mountain (25:9, 40).

The prophet Isaiah saw in his inaugural vision the Lord present in the temple and the seraphim worshiping God in hymnody:

> In the year that King Uzziah died, I saw the Lord sitting on a throne, high and lofty; and the hem of his robe filled the temple. Seraphs were in attendance above him; each had six wings: with two they covered their faces, and with two they covered their feet, and with two they flew. And one called to another and said:
> "Holy, holy, holy is the Lord of hosts;
> the whole earth is full of his glory" (6:1-3).

The prophet Ezekiel saw in a series of visions the glory of the Lord (that is, God's presence) departing from the temple in Jerusalem because of Israel's iniquities and then returning; the prophet was instructed that the return of God's glory would come when Israel was ready to conform to the heavenly pattern of the temple and its worship:

> Then the glory of the Lord went forth from the threshold of the house, and stood over the cherubim. And the cherubim lifted up their wings and mounted up from the earth in my sight as they went forth, with the wheels beside them; and they stood at the door of the east gate of the house of the Lord; and the glory of the Lord of Israel was over them (10:18-19).

> Afterward he brought me to the gate, the gate facing east. And behold, the glory of the God of Israel came from the east; and the sound of his coming was like the sound of many waters; and the earth shone with his glory.... As the glory of the Lord entered the temple by the gate facing east, the Spirit lifted me up, and brought me into the inner court; and behold, the glory of the Lord filled the temple (43:1-3, 4-5).

> "And you, son of man, describe to the house of Israel the temple that they may measure its pattern, that they may be ashamed of their iniquities. And if they are ashamed of all that they have done, portray the form of the temple, its arrangements, its exits, and its whole form; and make known to them all its ordinances and its laws; and write it down in their sight, so that they may observe and perform its whole form and all its ordinances" (43:10-11).

This material gave rise to a Jewish mystical tradition which saw the worship of the temple as a reflection of the heavenly liturgy. Isaiah's vision may echo the hymnody of the temple in his day, and some early versions of the Sanctus in Christian use may incorporate expanded texts of Isaiah's hymn used first in the temple and then in the synagogue, as we shall see below.

In much of the Jewish apocalyptic thought of Jesus' day, however, the temple and its worship was rejected because it did not conform to the archetype of the temple in heaven and its worship. Only in the last days will the true temple be revealed, but it already exists in the heavens. The present worship of God's people must conform to the worship of heaven. This theology lies behind the cult as it was practiced at Qumran, which was understood as participation through hymnody in the angelic liturgy of heaven.[1]

We find this apocalyptic perspective transposed into Christian terms in the prophetic visions of John the Divine. In several of these visions the seer is transported into the worship of heaven. In Revelation there is no longer a temple in heaven, for in the New Jerusalem access to God needs no mediation:

> I saw no temple in the city, for its temple is the Lord God Almighty and the Lamb. And the city has no need of sun or moon to shine on it, for the glory of God is its light, and its lamp is the lamb (21:22-23).

In several of the the visions, the seer beholds the liturgy of the heavenly city:

> At once I was in the spirit, and there in heaven stood a throne, with one seated on the throne. And the one seated there looks like jasper and carnelian, and around the throne is a rainbow that looks like an emerald. Around the throne are twenty-four thrones, and seated on the thrones are twenty-four elders, dressed in white robes, with golden crowns on their heads.... Around the throne, and on each side of the throne, are four living creatures.... And the four living creatures, each of them with six wings, are full of eyes all around and inside. Day and night without ceasing they sing,
> "Holy, holy, holy,
> the Lord God the Almighty,
> who was and is and is to come."

> And whenever the living creatures give glory and honor and thanks to the one who is seated on the throne, who lives forever and ever, the twenty-four elders fall before the one who is seated on the throne and worship the one who lives forever and ever; they cast their crowns before the throne, singing,
> "You are worthy, our Lord and God,
> to receive glory and honor and power,
> for you created all things,
> and by your will they exist and were created" (4:1-4, 6b, 8-11).

> After this I looked, and there was a great multitude that no one could count, from every nation, from all tribes and peoples and languages, standing before the throne and before the lamb, robed in white, with palm branches in their hands. They cried out in a loud voice saying,
> "Salvation belongs to our God who is seated on the throne,
> and to the Lamb!"

> And all the angels stood around the throne and around the elders and the four living creatures, and they fell on their faces before the throne and worshiped God, singing,
> "Amen! Blessing and glory and wisdom
> and thanksgiving and honor and power and might
> be to our God forever and ever! Amen " (7:9-12).

We note that the worship of heaven includes the hymn that Isaiah heard in the temple, which would enter Christian liturgy as the Sanctus.

It is the Letter to the Hebrews which presents the worship of the church as a participation in this heavenly liturgy. Much of the letter is taken up with the themes of the high priesthood of Jesus and the worship of the heavenly sanctuary:

> Now the main point of what we are saying is this: we have such a high priest [after the order of Melchizedek], one who is seated at the right hand of the Majesty in the heavens, a minister in the sanctuary and the true tabernacle that the Lord, and not any mortal, has set up. For every high priest is appointed to offer gifts and sacrifices; hence it is necessary for this priest also to have something to offer. Now if he were on earth, he would not be a priest at all, since there are priests who offer gifts according to the law. They offer worship in a sanctuary that is a sketch and shadow of the heavenly one; for Moses, when he was about to erect the tabernacle, was warned, "See that you make everything according to the pattern that was shown you on the mountain." But Jesus has now obtained a more excellent ministry, and to that degree he is the mediator of a better covenant...(8:1-6).
>
> For Christ did not enter into a sanctuary made by human hands, a mere copy of the true, but he entered into heaven itself, now to appear in the presence of God on our behalf.... But as it is, he has appeared once for all at the end of the age to remove sin by the sacrifice of himself....And it is by God's will that we have been sanctified through the offering of the body of Jesus Christ once for all (9:24, 26b; 10:10).
>
> You have not come to something that can be touched, a blazing fire, and darkness, and gloom, and a tempest, and the sound of a trumpet, and a voice whose words made the hearers beg that not another word be spoken to them.... But you have come to Mount Zion and to the city of the living God, the heavenly Jerusalem, and to innumerable angels in festal gathering, and to the assembly of the firstborn who are enrolled in heaven, and to God the judge of all, and to the spirits of the righteous made perfect, and to Jesus the mediator of a new covenant...(12:18-19, 22-24a).
>
> We have an altar from which those who officiate in the tabernacle have no right to eat. For the bodies of those animals whose blood is brought into the sanctuary for sin are burned outside the camp. Therefore Jesus also suffered outside the city gate in order to sanctify the people by his own blood. Let us then go to him outside the camp and bear the abuse he endured. For here we have no lasting city, but we are looking for the city that is to come. Through him, then, let us continually offer a sacrifice of praise to God, that is the fruit of lips that confess his name (11:10-15).

The church at worship is thus understood to be united with Jesus who has presented his sacrifice on our behalf before the throne of grace in heaven.

THE USE OF THE *QEDUSHAH* (SANCTUS) IN JEWISH *BERAKOTH*

At some time after the destruction of the temple the hymn of the seraphim from Isaiah's vision was incorporated in two of the key prayer texts of the Jewish synagogue—the *Yotzer*, the first of the *berakoth* on the *Shema*, and the *Qedushah*, the third of the *berakoth* of the *Tefillah*, the series of intercessory blessings recited three times a day. Here are the texts of these two *berakoth*:

Yotzer (First *Berakah* before the *Shema*)

Blessed art thou, O Lord our God, King of the universe, "who dost form the light and create the darkness" (Isaiah 45:7); who sheddest the light of thy mercy upon the earth and those who dwell on it; who, out of goodness, dost constantly renew every day the works of thy creation.

"How splendid are thy works, O Lord! Thou hast done them all with wisdom; earth is full of thy riches" (Psalm 104:24). Sublime king, the one and only from before time, glorious, magnificent, exalted since the days of eternity!

God of the universe, in accordance with thy many mercies, take pity on us, sovereign Lord of our strength, rock of our refuge, shield of our salvation, our refuge!

The blessed God in his great wisdom prepared and formed the rays of the sun. He created this good thing for the glory of his name. He set the stars in place in accordance with his power. The leaders of his armies are his holy ones. Ceaselessly they extol God, they proclaim the glory of the Almighty and his holiness. Blessed art thou, O Lord our God, for the splendid work of thy hands and for the lamps that thou hast created. May they glorify thee!

Blessed art thou, our rock, our king, our redeemer, who createst the holy ones. May thy name be glorified for eternity, our king, who createst the angels! Thine angels stand in the heights of heaven; together, in a loud voice, they proclaim with reverence the works of the living God and king of the universe. All of them are holy, all chosen, all powerful; with respect and reverence all do the will of their Creator; all open their mouths in holiness and purity, they sing melodiously, they bless, they glorify, they magnify, they adore, they proclaim the holy king and the name of God...They say with reverence:
"Holy, holy, holy is the Lord Sabaoth!
The earth is full of his glory" (Isaiah 6:3).

And the wheels and the holy living creatures, with a thunderous noise, rise up to face one another; they give glory and say:
"Blessed be the glory of the Lord
in the place where he dwells" (Ezekiel 3:12).

To the blessed God they offer their songs; to the God who is king, living and eternal, they sing hymns and proclaim his praises. For he alone does wonders and accomplishes new things, this master of battles. He sows justice, makes salvation bear fruit, creates healings. He is revered that he may be praised, the Lord of wonders.

Out of goodness he ceaselessly renews, every day, the works of his creation, as it is said: "He creates the great lamps, for his love is everlasting" (Psalm 136:7). Illumine Zion with a new light! Let us soon be made worthy of thy light! Blessed art thou, O Lord, who createst the stars.

Qedushah (Third Berakah of the Tefillah)

The multitudes of heaven crown thee, together with the congregations here below. Together they will thrice proclaim thy holiness, as the prophet says: "They were crying out to one another and singing:
Holy, holy, holy, the Lord Sabaoth.
The earth is full of his glory!" (Isaiah 6:3).

Then, with the crash of resounding thunder, marvelous and mighty, they will make their voices heard and, rising toward thee, they will say:
"Blessed be the glory of the Lord
in thy dwelling place!" (Ezekiel 3:12).

Shine forth from thy place, O our King, reign over us, for we await thee. When wilt thou reign? Reign in Zion soon, in our days. In our lifetime establish thy dwelling. Be glorified and sanctified in the midst of Jerusalem, thy city, from generation to generation and for ever. May our eyes see thy reign, according to the word that was said in the songs of thy power through the mouth of David, the One Anointed with thy justice:
"The Lord will reign for ever,
thy God, O Zion, from age to age!
Alleluia!" (Psalm 146:10).

From generation to generation we proclaim the kingdom of God, for he alone is the Most High, the Holy One. May the proclamation of thy glory, O our God, never leave our lips, for thou art the great King, thou art the Holy One. Blessed art thou, O Lord, holy God![2]

The shock of the disappearance of the sacrificial cult in Judaism after the destruction of the temple by the Romans led to the reorganization of Jewish worship in a form which we know as rabbinic Judaism. The daily sacrifices and the forms of worship at the temple appointed for the great pilgrimage festivals (Passover, Pentecost, and Tabernacles) and the day of atonement had to be transposed into other forms of worship. This transposition had already taken place before the destruction of the temple in those forms of sectarian Judaism that rejected the temple of the first century as a corrupt institution. We see in the incorporation of the seraphic hymn and related material into these two key texts of the liturgy of the synagogue one aspect of this transposition. It appears that the hymn was first incorporated into the *Yotzer* and from there migrated at a later date into the *Tefillah* (where it is used only in corporate recitation of the prayers).

THE SANCTUS BECOMES PART OF THE EUCHARISTIC PRAYER

The Jewish table blessings which are the prototype of the eucharistic prayer make no use of the Sanctus. But in the early stages of Christian worship, the liturgy of the table was joined to a liturgy of the word which resembles the sabbath service of the Jewish synagogue. This development was surely precipitated in part by the expulsion of Christians from the synagogue and the evolution of the church from its early status as a variant form of Judaism to its later status as a distinct religious body. By the time of Justin Martyr in the mid-second century we find the two liturgies joined in the worship of the church on the Lord's Day.

For those Christians who lived in close association with Judaism (in the Middle East and in Egypt and parts of North Africa) elements of Jewish prayer from the liturgy of the synagogue would be a natural component of such a Sunday service. The custom of reading Scripture is the most obvious component of the sabbath service which the Christians adapted. Another is the form of intercessory prayer represented by the *Tefillah* of the synagogue and the litany of Eastern rites. Since both Jews and Christians understood their worship as a participation in the heavenly liturgy, the Sanctus was another element which it was natural to borrow. In the fourth century we find it beginning to be incorporated in the eucharistic prayer—that is, it has moved from the Christian analogue of the liturgy of the synagogue to the Christian analogue of the table blessings. Our earliest witnesses are in West Syrian regions (Cyril of Jerusalem and Theodore of Mopsuestia); the Sanctus also made an early appearance in Egypt. The use of the Sanctus spread rapidly, but it was several centuries before it became a standard part of the eucharistic prayer. Latin Christians appear to have been tardy in catching up to the trend. When the Sanctus did appear, it was incorporated in different ways. At times it seems to have simply been prefaced to the eucharistic prayer; at other times it was inserted into the body of the prayer; in

Alexandria it seems to have been appended to the prayer. At times it seems to have taken with it part of the text in which it was embedded in the liturgy of the synagogue.

THE EUCHARISTIC PRAYERS OF CYRIL OF JERUSALEM AND THEODORE OF MOPSUESTIA

In the fourth century, as crowds of converts were seeking baptism in a newly Christian empire, bishops adopted the strategy of preparing these candidates by instructing them on the Christian faith during Lent and on the meaning of Christian worship in the week after Easter baptisms. The series of homilies on the rites of initiation which were delivered by Cyril of Jerusalem (or his successor John) and by Theodore of Mopsuestia in the East and by Ambrose of Milan in the West are among the most useful documentation available to us for worship during this period.

By the end of this century Christianity, which had been a persecuted counterculture for more than two centuries, had become the dominant culture. Bishops of the great sees of the church were often men trained in schools of Greek and Roman rhetoric. It was a time of immense liturgical creativity and innovation and of considerable theological ferment. Liturgical traditions of the great sees borrowed from each other, and local diversity gave way to a measure of uniformity. The earlier practice of improvising prayer within a relatively fixed thematic framework gave way to fixed liturgical texts, and the rites of patriarchal sees gradually supplanted variant rites within their regions. In the process, a relatively standard framework or outline for the anaphora emerged, creating what we think of as the West Syrian pattern for the eucharistic prayer. But this pattern evolved out of earlier patterns. We can see this evolution in process in the homilies of Cyril and Theodore.

When scholars first began to examine the liturgical data in their homilies, they brought to their analysis presuppositions based on the text of later West Syrian anaphoras—such as those attributed to Basil of Caesarea, John Chrysostom, and James of Jerusalem. Trying to fit the standard West Syrian pattern for eucharistic prayers to the commentaries found in the baptismal homilies of Cyril and Theodore proved a perplexing task, however, for the anaphoras sketched out in those homilies do not appear to conform to the pattern.

This is clearest in the case of Cyril's homilies, for he gives a quite specific description of the eucharistic prayer. If we compare it with the standard outline of later West Syrian prayers, the problem becomes clear. Let us set the two outlines in parallel tables:

Cyril's Fifth Baptismal Homily	West Syrian Anaphoras
Preliminary dialogue (Sursum corda)	Preliminary dialogue (Sursum corda)
Preface (Praise of God)	Preface (Praise of God)
Pre-Sanctus	Pre-Sanctus
Sanctus	Sanctus
	Post Sanctus (Christological Thanksgiving)
	Institution Narrative
	Anamnesis/Oblation
[Oblation? and] Epiclesis	Epiclesis
Intercessions	Intercessions

The bold-faced elements in the right-hand column are absent from Cyril's description. Many scholars find it so unlikely that these elements were missing from Cyril's eucharistic prayer that they try to explain away their absence in the fifth homily. But the most obvious explanation is that which Dix offers: Cyril made no mention of these elements because they were not part of his eucharistic prayer.[3]

There are several other features of Cyril's anaphora that we should note. The praise of God in the preface appears to focus strongly on God as creator. Thematically his preface resembles the material which introduces the Sanctus in the *Yotzer*, although there does not seem to be a verbal dependence on that text. What is particularly striking is the absence of any reference to Christ in the thanksgiving as Cyril describes it. The language of sacrifice has become more pronounced in Cyril: he refers to the eucharist as a "spiritual sacrifice," an "unbloody service," a "propitiatory sacrifice." It seems likely that he is echoing the language of the eucharistic prayer, but it is not clear just where in the text of the prayer that reference is to be found. Below I will suggest that an oblation is made in the introduction to the epiclesis. Ordinarily the supplication in early eucharistic prayers was for the church and the communicants: here it covers the whole range of intentions found in most rites in the prayers of the people of the liturgy of the word. Cyril justifies this practice (which he may have introduced in the rite of Jerusalem) by arguing that "we believe that these souls will obtain the greatest help if we make our prayers for them while the holy and most awesome sacrifice is being offered."[4] A characteristic formulation of intercessions in the West Syrian tradition from this time on will be, "we offer this sacrifice for...." The most striking claim in Cyril's commentary is the way in which he describes the sacrifice that is offered: "we offer Christ who has been slain for our sins, and so we appease the merciful God both on their behalf [that of the departed] and on ours."[5] Such a claim to offer Christ in sacrifice is rare in this period. Earlier language of sacrifice spoke of a sacrifice of thanksgiving and even associated the offerings of bread and wine with this sacrifice, but no association was made with the sacrifice of Christ. Cyril can make this association because he believes that the church's offering has been united with Christ's sacrifice.

Cyril's rite is grounded in the church's participation in the heavenly liturgy. This finds expression in the church's participation in the Sanctus: Cyril declares that we join in this hymn "so that we may share with the supernatural armies in their hymnody."[6] This perspective reflects the passages from Hebrews cited above: in the eucharist we "have come to Mount Zion and to the city of the living God, the heavenly Jerusalem, and to innumerable angels in festal gathering, and to the assembly of the firstborn who are enrolled in heaven, and to God the judge of all, and to the spirits of the righteous made perfect, and to Jesus the mediator of a new covenant...." As the church, having "lifted up our hearts" and approached the heavenly altar, we sanctify ourselves as we join in the seraphic hymn.

This hymn is followed, according to Cyril, by the invocation of the Holy Spirit, whose function as he articulates it is to ask God to join our offerings on the church's altar to Christ's sacrifice at the heavenly altar, "that he may make the bread the body of Christ and the wine the blood of Christ."[7] This way of understanding the church's participation in the heavenly liturgy follows the logic of Hebrews, but goes beyond what is suggested in the text of that letter. In Jewish texts the citation of the seraphic hymn has something of an epicletic function, and in some early anaphoras (see the analysis of the anaphora of St. Mark in chapter 4) an epiclesis is associated with the Sanctus as a kind of embolism on that hymn. From this perspective the offering of the bread and wine as figures of Christ body and blood unites them to the one sacrifice which he pleads before the heavenly altar and so, as Cyril says, "completes" the church's sacrifice.[8] But not many in this period would then go on to say that "we offer Christ."

An issue which we have not yet addressed is that raised by the prior baptismal homily in Cyril's series. That homily is an exposition of the meaning of communion grounded in an exegesis of the account of the last supper. While the eucharistic prayer of Cyril's church provided a good basis for his exposition of the theology of the eucharistic sacrifice, it furnished a less adequate basis for his exposition of the meaning of communion. And so he set out that theology in a separate homily, where his text is not the eucharistic prayer but an account of the last supper. While he attributes the account to Paul, the texts he cites in fact have significant variants from chapter 11 of 1 Corinthians. He is perhaps citing that account as it has been modified in liturgical usage, for in his various periods of exile from Jerusalem Cyril almost certainly encountered anaphoras which included an account of the institution (as Jerusalem's anaphora would before long). Here too he works with a typological perspective, as he would do in treating the eucharistic worship of the church as a figure of the heavenly liturgy. But here it is the bread and wine which are figures—figures of the body and blood of Christ which will enable the communicants to become participants in the body and blood of Christ and so partakers of the divine nature. To make this argument he needs an account of the last supper, and since his anaphora does not have one, he treats that account in a separate homily.

Theodore's homilies present us with a more complex picture. Theodore prefaces each homily with a synopsis of the rite to be discussed as that rite has come down to him in the tradition of the church. If we analyze the synopsis prefaced to the homily on the eucharistic celebration, the structure of the eucharistic prayer which is set out is exactly the same as we find in Cyril's fifth catechesis. But it appears that the rite which Theodore uses has evolved beyond the rite which he first received in the tradition. The rite given in the synopsis is characterized by Theodore as established by "the law of the church"; the rite which he expounds has further features established by "the law of the priesthood."[9] This latter term apparently designates the decisions of episcopal authority in establishing the shape of the eucharistic prayer which celebrants are to use. Theodore's prose is somewhat prolix, and it is far from easy to determine the exact shape of the prayer which he is describing in the body of the homily, but it is clear that it has a post-Sanctus that narrates the economy of Christ's saving deeds and has either a citation of Christ's institution of the eucharist or the account of the institution. The table below sets out the rites of "the law of the church" and "the law of the priesthood":

The Law *(Nomos)* of the Church	The Law *(Nomos)* of the Priesthood
Preliminary dialogue (*Sursum corda*)	Preliminary dialogue (*Sursum corda*)
Preface (Praise of God)	Preface (Praise of God)
Pre-Sanctus	Pre-Sanctus
Sanctus	**Post Sanctus (Narrative of the "Economy")**
	Reference to Baptism and Eucharist
[Oblation? and] Epiclesis	Epiclesis
Intercessions	Intercessions[10]

Theodore's fuller form of the anaphora also incorporates explicit trinitarian references. It is unclear how many of the standard West Syrian components Theodore has included after the Sanctus. The post-Sanctus seems to include *references* to the institution of both baptism and the eucharist (as do the various forms of the anaphora of St. Basil), but it unclear whether there was an institution account and anamnesis as well.

For Theodore as for Cyril the church's offering is a figure of the heavenly liturgy in which the church participates. But Theodore's text moves farther than Cyril in its understanding of the heavenly liturgy, for the three-fold "Holy" of the seraphic hymn is understood as a revelation of the Trinity. The interpretation of the eucharistic sacrifice also takes on a whole new dimension in Theodore's commentary, for he sees in the unfolding of the rite a figurative representation of Christ's death, burial, and resurrection—an interpretation which finds no warrant in the text itself.

RECONSTRUCTING THE EUCHARISTIC PRAYER OF THE JERUSALEM CHURCH

John Fenwick has done a careful analysis of the anaphora of St. James, which is the patriarchal rite of the church in Jerusalem.[11] He argues that what we have in this anaphora is a fusion of the earlier liturgy of the patriarchal see, as witnessed in Cyril's baptismal homilies and the sermon of Eusebius of Caesarea at the dedication of a church in Antioch, and the newer components of the West Syrian anaphoral pattern, borrowed from the earliest form of the anaphora of St. Basil. While there are further embellishments to the prayer, Fenwick believes that we can discover with reasonable certainty an approximate text of the prayer on which Cyril comments in his baptismal homily by removing from the Syriac text of the prayer the material borrowed from Basil. The result would be something like the following:

It is truly fitting and right, suitable and profitable, to praise thee, to bless thee, to worship thee, to glorify thee, to give thanks to thee, the creator of all creation, visible and invisible. Thou art hymned by the heaven of heavens and all their powers, by the sun and moon and all the choir of stars, by earth, sea, and all that is in them; by the heavenly Jerusalem, the church of the first-born written in heaven, by angels, archangels, thrones, dominions, principalities and powers, and awesome virtues. The cherubim with many eyes and seraphim with six wings, who cover their own faces with two wings and their feet with two and fly with two, cry aloud to one another with unwearying mouths and never silent hymns of praise and with clear voice the triumphal hymn of thy magnificent glory, proclaiming, praising, crying, and saying:

Holy, holy, holy, Lord God of Sabaoth. Heaven and earth are full of thy glory. Hosanna in the highest. Blessed is the one that has come and comes in the name of the Lord. Hosanna in the highest.

We therefore offer thee this awesome and bloodless sacrifice, that thou wouldst not deal with us according to our sins nor reward us according to our iniquities, but according to thy loving kindness and love for humankind wouldst blot out the sins of thy suppliants, for thy people and thy church entreats thee:

Have mercy upon us, almighty Father.

Have mercy upon us, God the Father almighty, and send out upon us and upon these gifts set before thee thy Holy Spirit, *the Lord and giver of life, who with thee and thy Son is enthroned and reigns, consubstantial and coeternal, who spoke by the law and the prophets and in thy new covenant, who descended in the likeness of a dove upon our Lord Jesus Christ at the river Jordan, who descended upon thy holy apostles in the likeness of fiery tongues,* that he may descend upon them, and make this bread the holy body of Christ and this cup the precious blood of Christ, that they may avail to all who partake of them for sanctification of souls and bodies, for strengthening thy holy catholic church, which thou didst found upon the rock of faith, that the gates of hell should not prevail against it, rescuing it from every heresy, and from the stumbling blocks of those who work lawlessness until the consummation of the age.

We offer to thee for…[*Extensive intercessions and a doxology conclude the prayer.*][12]

Fenwick believes that this text may represent an intermediate stage between the text which Cyril inherited and the final form. He believes that Cyril himself may have added the epiclesis and the intercessions. It is likely that Cyril was responsible for the expanded intercession, and it is possible that he added the epiclesis, but it is also quite possible that some form of epiclesis was already attached to the Sanctus (as we see in the Alexandrian tradition). In any case the italicized attributes of the

Spirit in the epiclesis seem unlikely to have been in the text that Cyril inherited. They are paralleled in Cyril's catecheses on the creed, but in the epiclesis itself they probably represent a later embellishment.

To this material the final redactor of the anaphora added from the Alexandrian anaphora of St. Basil the material required to conform to the standard West Syrian pattern for eucharistic prayers. He also expanded the intercessions further, using material from Basil and elsewhere. We will return to consider the final form of this anaphora in chapter 3.

NOTES

[1] On all of this see Mazza, *Origins of the Eucharistic Prayer*, pages 210-217. There is an extensive literature on the Sanctus. For recent discussion, see Bryan Spinks, *The Sanctus in the Eucharistic Prayer* (Cambridge, 1991).

[2] Translation of texts, with adaptation, from Lucien Deiss, *The Springtime of the Liturgy* (Collegeville: Liturgical Press, 1979), pages 12-13, 15-16.

[3] Dix, *The Shape of the Liturgy*, page 198. For the discussion which follows, see Enrico Mazza, *The Origins of the Eucharistic Prayer* (Collegeville: Liturgical Press, 1995), excursus to chapter 5 (Theodore of Mopsuestia) and chapter 8 (Theodore and Cyril).

[4] Ibid., 9.

[5] Fifth mystagogical catechesis, 10.

[6] Ibid., 6.

[7] Ibid., 7.

[8] Ibid., 8.

[9] See Mazza, *The Origins of the Eucharistic Prayer*, page 205, for this distinction.

[10] This is my adaptation of the table given by Mazza, *The Origins of the Eucharistic Prayer*, page 309.

[11] John Fenwick, *The Anaphoras of St. Basil and St. James: An Investigation of their Common Origin* (Rome: Pontificium Institutum Orientale, 1992).

[12] The text here is based on the Latin translation of the Syriac text which is printed in John Fenwick, *The Anaphoras of St. Basil and St. James: An Investigation of their Common Origin.* Fenwick prints it in parallel with the (longer) Greek text. An English translation of the text of St. James (with the additional material of the Greek text indicated as bracketed material) may be found in Jasper and Cuming, *Prayers of the Eucharist: Early and Reformed,* pages 90-99. I have omitted the second invocation of the Holy Spirit in the epiclesis, which is not found in the Greek text and is probably a later accretion.

CHAPTER THREE

THE WEST SYRIAN STANDARD
HIPPOLYTUS AND THE LITURGIES OF ST. BASIL,
ST. JOHN CHRYSOSTOM, AND ST. JAMES

❖ ❖ ❖ ❖ ❖ ❖ ❖ ❖ ❖ ❖ ❖ ❖ ❖

THE *APOSTOLIC TRADITION* ATTRIBUTED
TO HIPPOLYTUS

Church orders are a unique genre of early Christian literature. They are manuals for the life of the church with catechetical, discipli-nary, and liturgical material purporting to be based in apostolic or even dominical mandates. The earliest of the church orders is the document that we studied in chapter 1, the *Didache*, whose full title is the *Teaching (Didache) of the Twelve Apostles*. The next in the series is a work attributed to Hippolytus of Rome and known as the *Apostolic Tradition*. Later manuals of this kind are the *Didascalia (Teaching) of the Apos-tles,* the *Apostolic Constitutions*, and the *Testament of the Lord (Testa-mentum Domini)*. It is not at all clear that all these manuals were adopt-ed by significant Christian communities: many seem to have been set forth as programs of reform by their authors or compilers. The implic-it claims escalate as time goes on. The earliest of them simply claim to be rooted in apostolic teaching or tradition; the *Apostolic Constitutions* attributes various parts of its program to individual apostles; the *Testamentum Domini* claims to be nothing less than the legacy of Christ.

By the fifth century the church orders were all obsolete; churches were confident enough to set forth their own programs without resorting to claiming direct apostolic warrant for what they were doing.[1]

The *Apostolic Tradition* is a key document in these manuals: large portions of it were incorporated into the *Apostolic Constitutions* and the *Testamentum Domini*. This document, originally written in Greek, has had to be reconstructed from later manuals into which it was incorporated. Often these manuals survive only in later translations into other languages. The *Apostolic Tradition* is generally dated in the early third century. Most scholars attribute it to Hippolytus, a Roman presbyter, who was an opponent of the dominant party in the Roman church in his era. It appears to represent his program for the Roman church, rooted in apostolic tradition rather than the innovations which he opposes in the church of his day.

Its Roman provenance as well as its attribution to Hippolytus have been disputed. Its baptismal practice is certainly Roman: its initiatory rites are distinctly Roman in character and are reflected in later Roman practice. But the sample eucharistic prayer which Hippolytus offers as a model for use at ordinations cannot be considered as the ancestor of the later Roman canon. This eucharistic prayer has had an enormous influence in the twentieth century, for it is the earliest text of a eucharistic prayer to have come down to us. But in Christian antiquity the model which Hippolytus offered for a eucharistic prayer found its successors not in Rome, but in Greek-speaking Syrian churches and in Ethiopia, where it remains in use under the title "the Anaphora of the Apostles." This anaphora preserves the eucharistic prayer of the *Apostolic Tradition* largely intact, but conforms it to the pattern of Alexandrian anaphoras by inserting into the initial thanksgiving a set of intercessions and the Sanctus. The text of the eucharistic prayer then resumes with a verbal link to the Sanctus resembling that which we find in the anaphora of St. Mark, but in this case the text does not take the form of an epiclesis. The epiclesis of the *Apostolic Tradition* is reworked so that it takes a consecratory form.[2] While this anaphora is not presently used in the Coptic Church of Egypt, its use in Ethiopia testifies to the earlier influence of the *Apostolic Tradition* in this region. We find earlier evidence of this influence in the *Canons of Hippolytus* and the *Egyptian Church Order*, both of which incorporate material from the *Apostolic Tradition*.

The text of this prayer does not survive in Greek, but only in translation. This presents problems only in the text of the invocation of the Spirit at the end of the prayer, which we must reconstruct from variant versions. The prayer begins with the eucharistic dialogue in the form which became traditional in the West and continued as follows:

> We give thanks to thee, O God, through thy beloved child [*puer* = *pais*] Jesus Christ, whom in the last times thou didst send to us as a savior and redeemer and angel of your will; who is thine inseparable Word, through whom thou didst make all things, and in whom thou wert well pleased, [whom] thou didst send from heaven into a virgin's womb and who, dwelling in the womb, was made flesh and manifested as thy Son, born of the Holy Spirit and the virgin; who, fulfilling thy will and purchasing for thee a holy people, stretched out his hands when he suffered, that he might deliver from suffering those who believed in thee; who, when he was handed over to his voluntary suffering that he might destroy death and break the bonds of the devil and tread down hell and shine upon the righteous and set a bound and manifest the resurrection, took bread and gave thanks and said, "Take, eat; this is my body, which shall be broken for you;" and likewise also the cup, saying, "This is my blood, which is shed for you. When you do this you do it in remembrance of me."
>
> Remembering therefore his death and resurrection, we offer to thee the bread and the cup, giving thanks to thee that thou hast accounted us worthy to stand before thee and minister to thee.
>
> And we ask that thou wouldst send thy Holy Spirit upon the offering of thy holy church, and that, gathering it into one, thou would grant to all the holy ones who partake [to do so] for the fulness of the Holy Spirit, for the strengthening of faith in truth, that we may praise and glorify thee through thy child [*puer* = *pais*] Jesus Christ; through whom be glory and honor to thee, to the Father and the Son with the Holy Spirit in thy holy church, both now and for ever. Amen.[3]

This is a tripartite text, like the *Birkat ha-Mazon*. We have two paragraphs of thanksgiving and a concluding supplication.[4] The first thanksgiving is quite long: it is usually printed as two paragraphs, but it is really one sentence, consisting of a long series of relative clauses. The narrative of the institution comes in the last clause of this series. The second paragraph (as the text is divided here), which includes the anamnesis and offering, takes the form of a second brief thanksgiving. What we customarily call the epiclesis or invocation is found in the last paragraph, which is a supplication for the communicants as the church.

Notice the elements added to the earlier texts found in the *Didache*. The first thanksgiving incorporates a relatively extensive narrative of the economy of salvation in Christ. The institution narrative is not structurally independent, but forms the last relative clause of the first thanksgiving. An anamnesis and offering are linked to the institution narrative, but take the form of a second thanksgiving. Finally, the epiclesis in this case seems to have developed out of the supplication for the communicants as the church. Although the Spirit is invoked upon the elements, the invocation does not appear to have consecratory force, but has as its goal the unity and sanctification of the church. The Sanctus, which was the first addition to the primitive nucleus in the texts to which Cyril and Theodore bear witness (and probably in the expanded version of the anaphora of St. Mark which we will consider in the next chapter), is not part of the prayer of Hippolytus, and the first thanksgiving has only the briefest reference to creation.

THE EMERGENT WEST SYRIAN NORM

The eucharistic prayer of Hippolytus seems to have provided the basic structure for the Greek-speaking Christians of the Middle East,[5] where the dominant prayers to emerge were the anaphora of St. Basil (in its Egyptian and Byzantine forms), the anaphora of St. John Chrysostom (whose earlier form is known as the anaphora of the apostles), and the anaphora of St. James (which seems to have been constructed, as we have seen, out of the earlier eucharistic prayer of Jerusalem and the anaphora of St. Basil). But the earliest witness we have to the use of this basic structure is the anaphora found in the eighth book of the *Apostolic Constitutions*.

The author of that eucharistic prayer appears to have combined a brief local eucharistic prayer with that of Hippolytus and then expanded the material to enormous length:[6] the prayer did not remain in use long, if indeed it was ever used. Its author either works with an archaic Christology or is Arian in sympathy, and many versions of the prayer have edited out theologically suspect phrases. For the first time we find a prayer with the threefold creedal structure that would be characteristic of West Syrian prayers. Let us look at the shape of this prayer:

Preface, Pre-Sanctus, and Sanctus

Dialogue
Preface
    Praise of God
    Thanksgiving for Creation
    Thanksgiving for the Economy of the Old Covenant
Pre-Sanctus
Sanctus

Post-Sanctus, Institution Narrative, Anamnesis/Oblation/ Thanksgiving
Post-Sanctus: Thanksgiving for the Economy of Christ
Institution Narrative
Anamnesis/Oblation/ Thanksgiving

Supplication
Invocation (epiclesis) of the Spirit upon the gifts for the sanctification of communicants
Extensive intercessions
Final Doxology

The structure is really one of two thanksgivings and a supplication, but each section has been enormously expanded. The Sanctus forms the conclusion of the first thanksgiving; the institution narrative with its anamnesis and oblation form the conclusion of the second thanksgiving, which begins with the post-Sanctus; and the epiclesis opens the supplication. The post-Sanctus begins with the characteristic West Syrian link to the Sanctus—"Holy."

The value of the anaphora of the *Apostolic Constitutions*, which probably received little or no actual use, is the insight that it gives us into the evolution of the eucharistic prayer in this region.[7] We might outline that evolution as follows:[8]

First Stage: the Nucleus of the Anaphora
Brief Thanksgiving(s) and Supplication

Second Stage
Incorporation of the pre-Sanctus and Sanctus and perhaps an epiclesis (as in Cyril)

Third Stage
Addition of other elements
1. Narrative of the economy of salvation (distributed in different ways in different anaphoras in preface and post-Sanctus)

2. Institution narrative and Anamnesis/Oblation/Thanksgiving (conclusion of the post-Sanctus)
    Anamnesis/thanksgiving at Antioch
    Anamnesis/oblation in Basil

3. Consecratory invocation at beginning of supplication
    Some prayers have invocation of Spirit on both gifts and
        communicants
    Other prayers have invocation of Spirit on gifts alone

4. Incorporation of popular hymnodic acclamations
    penitential: "Have mercy" (Jerusalem)
    memorial: "We proclaim your death" (Jerusalem)
    doxological: "We praise you" (Antioch/Constantinople)

5. Trinitarian and Christological embellishments

THE ANAPHORAS OF THE APOSTLES AND OF JOHN CHRYSOSTOM

The "native" eucharistic prayer of Antioch appears to be the "Urtext" behind the present Byzantine anaphora attributed to St. John Chrysostom and the Syriac anaphora of the Twelve Apostles. Unlike other West Syrian anaphoras, it has a relatively brief narrative of the economy of salvation, and the greater part of this narrative is to be found in the preface, which moves rapidly from creation to the eschaton. Indeed, the text of the post-Sanctus after the linking "holy" consists only of the citation of John 3:16. The text of the two derivatives of this Urtext is substantially identical until the end of the anamnesis. It appears that from this point on the of each has been reworked: The anaphora of the apostles has probably incorporated material from Jerusalem and elsewhere and reworked its intercessions; the anaphora of St. John Chrysostom appears to have undergone several revisions—the anamnesis has been reworked, then the acclamation standard in Constantinople has been incorporated, and the intercessions have been reworked.

Let us set the texts of these two anaphoras in parallel columns[9] in order to compare them, marking differences in each text with italics:

Twelve Apostles	John Chrysostom
It is meet and right to worship thee *and to glorify thee*: for thou art *truly* God, thou and thine only-begotten Son and the Holy Spirit.	It is meet and right to *sing to thee, to bless thee, to praise thee, to give thanks to thee, to* worship thee *in all places of thy dominion*: for thou art God *ineffable, incomprehensible, invisible, unsearchable, eternal and unchanging*, thou and thine only-begotten Son and the Holy Spirit.
Thou didst bring us into being out of nothing, and when we had fallen into sin thou didst raise us up again, and thou didst not cease until thou hadst brought us unto heaven and hadst bestowed upon us thy kingdom to come. For all these things we give thanks to thee, and to thine only-begotten Son and the Holy Spirit.	Thou didst bring us into being out of nothing, and when we had fallen into sin thou didst raise us up again, and thou didst not cease until thou hadst brought us unto heaven and hadst bestowed upon us thy kingdom to come. For all these things we give thanks to thee, and to thine only-begotten Son and the Holy Spirit, *for all the benefits done for us, known or unknown, manifest or hidden.*
For cherubim with four faces and six-winged seraphim, with all the heavenly powers surround thee, glorifying with never-silent mouths and voices the praise of thy majesty, proclaiming, crying out, and saying:	*We give thanks to thee also because thou hast been pleased to receive this service at our hands, while thousands of archangels and tens of thousands of angels* surround thee, and with cherubim and six-winged *and many-eyed* seraphim, *borne aloft upon their wings,* cry out to one another with unceasing voice in unstilled hymns of glory:

Twelve Apostles

Holy, holy, holy, Lord of hosts! Heaven and earth are full of thy glory. Hosanna in the highest. Blessed is he that comes in the name of the Lord. Hosanna in the highest.

Holy and most holy art thou, and thine only-begotten Son and the Holy Spirit. Holy and most holy art thou, in thy glorious majesty, who didst so love the world that thou didst give thine only-begotten Son, that all who believe in him should not perish, but have everlasting life.

After he came and accomplished all that was ordained for our sakes, on the night in which he was given up, he took bread into his holy hands, *and when he had raised them to heaven he* blessed and hallowed and broke it and gave it to his disciples and apostles, saying, "Take, eat: this is my body, which is broken for you and for many and is given for the remission of sins *and for eternal life."*

Likewise the cup also after supper, *mixing wine and water, he gave thanks, blessed, hallowed, and after he had tasted it, gave it to his disciples and apostles,* saying, "Take, drink of this, all of you: This is the blood of the new covenant, which is shed for you and for many and is given for the remission of sins *and for eternal life. For as often as you eat this bread and drink this cup, you will proclaim my death until I come again."*

We commemorate thy death, O Lord, we confess thy resurrection, and we await thy second coming....

Remembering, therefore, thy saving command and all the things that came to pass for our sake, thy cross, thy resurrection from the dead on the third day, thy ascension to heaven and thy session at the right hand, and awaiting thy second and glorious coming again *in which thou wilt come in glory to judge the living and the dead, and to repay all humans according to their works in thy love for humankind—for thy church and thy flock beseech thee, saying through thee and with thee to thy Father, Have mercy upon me.*

John Chrysostom

Holy, holy, holy, Lord of hosts! Heaven and earth are full of thy glory. Hosanna in the highest. Blessed is he that comes in the name of the Lord. Hosanna in the highest.

And with these blessed powers, O Master, lover of humankind, we also cry out and say: Holy and most holy art thou, and thine only-begotten Son and the Holy Spirit. Holy and most holy art thou, in thy glorious majesty, who didst so love the world that thou didst give thine only-begotten Son, that all who believe in him should not perish, but have everlasting life.

After he came and accomplished all that was ordained for our sakes, on the night in which he was given up, *or rather gave himself up, for the life of the world,* he took bread into his *most pure and* holy *and spotless* hands, and when he had given thanks and blessed and hallowed it, he broke it and gave it to his *holy* disciples and apostles, saying, "Take, eat: this is my body, which is broken for you for the remission of sins."

Likewise the cup also after supper, saying, "Drink of this, all of you: This is my blood of the new covenant, which is shed for you and for many for the remission of sins."

Remembering, therefore, this saving command and all the things that came to pass for our sake, the cross, the grave, the resurrection on the third day, the ascension to heaven, the session at the right hand, and the second and glorious coming again:

Twelve Apostles	**John Chrysostom**

Have mercy upon us, O God the Father almighty, have mercy upon us.

We also, Lord, give thanks and confess thee in all and through all:

 we praise thee, bless thee, give thanks to thee, O Lord, and pray to thee, our God: [Be gracious, for thou art good, and have mercy upon all.]

We pray thee, therefore, *almighty Lord and God of the holy powers, falling down on our faces before thee,* that thou wouldst send thy Holy Spirit upon these gifts here set forth and *manifest* this bread as the *venerated* body of *our Lord Jesus* Christ and this cup the blood of *our Lord Jesus* Christ, that they may avail for those who partake of them *for life and resurrection,* for the remission of sins, for *health* of soul *and body,* for the communion of the Holy Spirit, *for enlightenment of mind, and for defence before the dread judgment-seat of thy Christ; and let none of thy people perish, Lord, but make us all worthy, that, serving thee without disturbance and ministering before thee at all times of our life, we may enjoy thy heavenly and immortal and life-giving mysteries, through thy grace and mercy and love for humankind, now and unto the ages of ages.*

We offer to thee this our reasonable service for *all humans, for thy catholic church, for the bishops in it who rightly divide the word of truth* ....:

---

bringing before thee thine own gifts from thine own creation in all and through all:

 we praise thee, bless thee, give thanks to thee, O Lord, and pray to thee, our God:

Again we offer to thee this reasonable and unbloody service. And we pray *and beseech and implore* thee, that thou wouldst send thy Holy Spirit upon these gifts here set forth and *make* this bread the body of thy Christ and *that which is in* this cup the precious blood of thy Christ, *transforming them by thy Holy Spirit* that they may avail for those who partake of them for *sobriety* of soul, for the remission of sins, for the communion of the Holy Spirit, *for the fulfilment of the kingdom of heaven, and for boldness before thee and not for judgment or condemnation.*

And again we offer to thee this our reasonable service for *all thy servants departed this life before us in the faith:*

Let us note, first of all, the trinitarian elaborations at the end of the preface and at the beginning of the post-Sanctus. This trinitarian reworking of a text is probably characteristic of the late fourth century; in this form it appears to be an Antiochene characteristic, for Theodore of Mopsuestia alludes to it in his description of the rite according to "the law of the church." Each anaphora has added embellishments of the text in certain places: note Chrysostom's attributes for God in the preface and the elaboration of the institution account in the Twelve Apostles. Note the phrase which is attached to the introduction to the Sanctus in Chrysostom, "We give thanks to thee also because thou hast been pleased to receive this service at our hands." The equivalent phrase in Twelve Apostles is found at the end of the epiclesis, not as a thanksgiving but as a petition. Its phraseology echoes the end of the anamnesis in the *Apostolic Tradition*: neither anaphora retains its original location in the eucharistic prayer.

The substantial differences start in the anamnesis. The first two acclamations and related material in Twelve Apostles appear to have been borrowed from the anaphora of St. James. The Syriac version of that anaphora, like the Syriac text of the Twelve Apostles, addresses the first acclamation and the anamnesis to Christ. The provenance of the third acclamation is difficult to discern: it does not appear to be native to Twelve Apostles, Chrysostom, or the anaphora of St. Basil, although all three now incorporate it.

It is difficult to be certain of the original form of the anamnesis.[10] The anamnesis in the *Apostolic Tradition* is coupled with both an oblation and a thanksgiving. It would appear that the Urtext of the two Antiochene anaphoras had a thanksgiving but no oblation, and that Chrysostom replaced the thanksgiving with an oblation to conform to the model of St. Basil. That would yield the following Antiochene Urtext and first redaction for Chrysostom, before the addition of the last two acclamations to Twelve Apostles and the one acclamation to John Chrysostom:

Antiochene Urtext	**John Chrysostom**
Remembering, therefore, this saving command and all the things that came to pass for our sake, the cross, the grave, the resurrection on the third day, the ascension to heaven, the session at the right hand, and the second and glorious coming again, we also, Lord, give thanks and confess thee.	Remembering, therefore, this saving command and all the things that came to pass for our sake, the cross, the grave, the resurrection on the third day, the ascension to heaven, the session at the right hand, and the second and glorious coming again, we offer to thee this reasonable and unbloody service.
And we pray thee, that thou wouldst send thy Holy Spirit upon these gifts here set forth…	And we pray thee, that thou wouldst send thy Holy Spirit upon these gifts here set forth…

Chrysostom appears initially to have suppressed the original thanksgiving in the anamnesis and to have replaced it with the characteristic formulation of the offering found in the supplication of the Urtext. A later redaction inserted the introduction to the acclamation found in Basil and so created a "double oblation," placing the oblation from Basil in the introduction to the acclamation and displacing Chrysostom's original oblation to a position immediately following the acclamation.

Twelve Apostles and Chrysostom have each elaborated the invocation of the Urtext. The clause asking for the transformation or change of the gifts is probably an addition to Chrysostom's first redaction of the Urtext; it is difficult to tell whether Twelve Apostles has elaborated the list of the fruits of communion at the end of the epiclesis or Chrysostom has abbreviated it. The intercessions of Twelve Apostles are relatively brief and probably close to the original of the Urtext: they take the characteristic form, "We offer to thee this our reasonable service for...." The intercessions begin with the commemoration of the living and conclude with the commemoration of the departed, with no sharp distinction between the saints and other departed Christians. In the present form of Chrysostom the sequence is reversed, with the commemoration of the departed coming first. Here the sequence of Chrysostom has been conformed to that of the Byzantine text of Basil, and the cue words from Basil to introduce the diptychs of the departed and the living have been incorporated into the text of Chrysostom. The intercessions have also been expanded; additional intercessions take the form characteristic of Basil, "Remember...."

THE EGYPTIAN AND BYZANTINE ANAPHORAS OF ST. BASIL

Basil of Caesarea was not Antiochene, but Cappadocian. His anaphora represents another branch of the West Syrian tradition. A whole series of variant recensions of an anaphora ascribed to him have come down to us. The most important are an Alexandrian recension which has survived in a Greek version and in translations into two Coptic dialects—Boharic and Sahidic—and the final Byzantine version which is still in use today. The Alexandrian anaphora ascribed to him is the shortest version of the text and, as Dom Hieronymus Engberding established in a study in 1932, the Sahidic version appears to be the earliest form of the anaphora for which we have manuscript witness.[11] Engberding's analysis focused on verbal comparisons only as far as the end of the post-Sanctus and took no account of the variants in the epiclesis and the intercessions. We might summarize the most important of his conclusions as follows:

> 1. The Alexandrian text represents a slight Egyptianization of Basil's original text, but is substantially the original Cappadocian text.

2. There was an intermediate form of the text which represents a first stage of redaction between the Alexandrian texts and the other versions that have come down to us. This stage is characterized by theological and biblical amplification of the text which are characteristic of the thought of Basil. Engberding gave this intermediate stage the name Ω-Basil.

John Fenwick expanded Engberding's analysis to the entire text of the anaphora and made structural as well as verbal comparisons.[12] The structural analysis of the intercessions modifies Engberding's conclusions somewhat. The first stage, best represented by the Syrian version, includes most of the amplifications to the body of the text up to the intercessions. The intercessions in Ω-Basil are amplified, but the original sequence is retained. Subsequently the intercessions were further amplified and the sequence reversed. The Armenian and Byzantine versions (which themselves differ from each other) derive from this second stage of redaction, which Fenwick calls ω-Basil. The history of the anaphora before the Alexandrian version of the text is difficult to establish. Basil must have had some hand in the text represented by the Alexandrian anaphora for it to be attributed to him. But he was undoubtedly working with the text for the prayer which came down to him in Cappadocian tradition, and we have no way of establishing what modifications he made in this text.

The text follows the standard West Syrian structure which is also characteristic of the Antiochene anaphora of the Twelve Apostles/ Chrysostom and the final form of the anaphora of St. James. That structure consists, as we have seen above, of three major sections: 1) preface/pre-Sanctus/Sanctus, 2) post-Sanctus/institution narrative/ anamnesis with oblation and/or thanksgiving, and 3) epiclesis/intercessions/ doxology. But the common structure disguises some significant differences. The brief preface of Twelve Apostles/Chrysostom really covers the entire economy of God, from creation to the eschaton. The post-Sanctus is little more than a link to the institution narrative, using the citation of John 3:16 to move from the link-word "holy" into the institution narrative. The anaphoras of Basil in all their versions restrict the preface to the praise of God and cover the entire economy of creation and redemption in the post-Sanctus, which is of substantial length.

Let us now look at these two recensions of the anaphora of Basil, picking up the text after the initial dialogue and marking text unique to each in italics:

The Alexandrian Anaphora: Preface, Pre-Sanctus, Sanctus

It is meet and right, meet and right, truly meet and right

[to give thanks to thee and to glorify thee,] thou who art, Master, Lord God *of truth, existing before the ages and reigning to the ages, dwelling in the heights and regarding the things below, who didst make heaven and the earth and the seas and all that is in them,* the Father of our Lord and God and Savior Jesus Christ, *through whom thou didst make all things,* visible and invisible *who* sits on the throne of *thy holy* glory.

O thou who art worshiped by every holy power, about whom stand angels, archangels, principalities and powers, and virtues: around thee stand also the many-eyed cherubim and the six-winged seraphim, *praising thee for all* and crying out and saying:

Holy, holy, holy, Lord of hosts! Heaven and earth are full of thy glory. Hosanna in the highest. Blessed is he that comes in the name of the Lord. Hosanna in the highest.

The Byzantine Anaphora: Preface, Pre-Sanctus, Sanctus

Thou who art, Lord and Master, God the Father almighty, worthy of worship: it is truly meet and right *and fitting to the majesty of thy holiness to praise thee, to sing to thee, to bless thee, to worship thee,* to give thanks to thee, to glorify thee, *who alone art truly God, and to offer thee with a contrite heart and a humble spirit this our reasonable service, for thou hast granted us the knowledge of thy truth. And who can tell thy mighty acts, or make thy praises heard, or tell of all thy wondrous deeds? O Master, Master of all and Lord of heaven and earth and of every creature,* visible and invisible, who sittest upon a throne of glory *and beholdest the depths, without beginning, invisible, incomprehensible, uncircumscribable, immutable, the unbegotten* Father of our Lord Jesus Christ, the *great* God and Savior. *He is our hope, the image of thy goodness, the seal bearing in himself the exact likeness that reveals thee, the Father, true God, eternal Wisdom, revealing the Father in himself, the Word of life, the true Light. Through him the Holy Spirit was manifested as the Spirit of truth, the grace of adoption, the earnest of our coming inheritance, the first-fruits of everlasting blessedness, the life-giving power, the fountain of sanctification, through whom every creature that has reason and understanding is enabled to worship thee and to render to thee an everlasting hymn of glory, for all things are subject to thee.*

Angels and archangels, *thrones and dominions,* principalities and powers, virtues and many-eyed cherubim praise thee. The six-winged seraphim, *veiling their faces with two wings and their feet with two wings and flying with two wings,* cry out to one another *with unceasing voice in unstilled hymns of glory:*

Holy, holy, holy, Lord of hosts! Heaven and earth are full of thy glory. Hosanna in the highest. Blessed is he that comes in the name of the Lord. Hosanna in the highest.

Post-Sanctus, Institution, Anamnesis

Holy, holy, holy indeed art thou, *O Lord our God,*

who didst form us and place *us* in the paradise of delight, and *when we had transgressed thy commandment and fallen from eternal life* through the deceit of the serpent and when we were cast out of the paradise *of delight,* thou didst not cast us off forever, but thou didst *continually* visit *us through* thy holy prophets,

Post-Sanctus, Institution, Anamnesis

And with these blessed powers, O Master, lover of humankind, we sinners also cry out and shout: Holy indeed *and all-holy* art thou, *and of the majesty of thy holiness there is no measure, and blessed art thou in all thy works, and thou didst bring all to pass for us in accordance with thy holy and righteous judgment.*

For thou didst form *the man out of dust taken from the ground and honor him, O God, with thine own image,* and place *him* in the paradise of delight, *promising him immortal life and the enjoyment of everlasting good things by keeping thy commandments. But when he did not heed thee, the true God who created him, and* through the deceit of the serpent *was led astray and doomed to death by his own transgressions,* thou, O God, *didst* cast *him* out *in thy just judgment from paradise into this world, and didst turn him again to the dust from which he was taken, providing him* salvation *through rebirth in thy Christ himself. For thou didst not abandon* forever *thy creature whom thou hadst made, O good one, nor didst thou forget the work of thy hands; but* thou didst visit *him in various ways out of thy merciful compassion.*

Thou didst send thy prophets; *thou didst do mighty works through thy saints who from generation to generation were well-pleasing to thee; thou didst speak to us through the mouths of thy servants the prophets, who foretold the salvation that was to come; thou didst give us the law to assist us; thou didst appoint guardian angels.*

Post-Sanctus, Institution, Anamnesis

And in these last days thou wert manifested to us through thine only Son, *our Lord and God and Savior Jesus Christ,*

who, having taken flesh of *the Holy Spirit and* the holy virgin *Mary and been made human,*

taught us the ways of salvation,

granting us to be born again by water *and the Holy Spirit, made* us a people of his own possession, and sanctified us by the Holy Spirit; who, *having loved his own who were in the world,* gave himself as a ransom to death *which reigned over us,* held in bondage, sold under sin. * And, having descended by the cross into hades, on the third day he rose again

[*The Sahidic text begins at this point. The preceding phrase "by his blood" differs from the Greek text.]

And, ascending into heaven, he sat down at the right of the Father, having appointed a day in which to judge the world and to render to all according to their works.

Post-Sanctus, Institution, Anamnesis

And when the fulness of time had come, thou didst speak to us through thine only Son, *by whom thou also didst make the worlds, who, being the brightness of thy glory and the express image of thy person and sustaining all things by the word of his power, did not think to grasp at equality with thee, O God and Father, but though he was eternal God he appeared upon earth and dwelt with humanity; and,* having taken flesh of the holy virgin, *he humbled himself and assumed the form of a servant, being made in the likeness of the body of our lowliness, that we might be made like the image of his glory: for since sin entered the world by a human being, and death by sin, thine only-begotten Son, who is in thy bosom, O God and Father, being born of a woman, the holy ever-virgin Mary, the bearer of God, being under the law, was pleased to condemn death in his own flesh, that those who were dead in Adam might be made alive in him, thy Christ. Dwelling in this world, he gave unto us* saving *commandments, and, having turned us from the deceits of idols, he brought us to the knowledge of thee, God and Father, the living and true, and purchased for himself* a people of his own possession, a royal priesthood, a holy nation. *He washed us with the cleansing of* water and sanctified us by the Holy Spirit, giving himself as a ransom to death, in which we were held in bondage, sold under sin. And, having descended by the cross into hades, *that he might fill all things with himself he loosed the pains of death; and on the third day he rose again and, having made a way for all flesh to the resurrection of the dead, since it was not possible that the prince of life should be held by corruption, he became the firstfruits of those who had fallen asleep, the first-born of the dead, that in all things he might have the primacy over all.* And, ascending into the heavens, he sat down at the right hand of thy Majesty on high, from which he shall come again to render to all according to their works.

He also left us *this great mystery of godliness*. For when he was about *to be handed over to* death, taking bread, blessing, hallowing, and breaking it, he *shared* it with his holy disciples and apostles, saying, "Take eat: this is my body, which is broken for you for the remission of sins. *Do this in remembrance of me.*" In the same way, he mingled the cup after supper, of wine and water, blessing and hallowing it, and giving thanks, he gave it to *them*, saying, "Drink this, all of you: this is my blood *of the new covenant*, which is poured out for you and for many for the remission of sins. Do this in remembrance of me: for whenever you eat this bread and drink this cup, you proclaim my death *until I come.*"

We also, remembering his *holy* passion and his resurrection from the dead, and his ascension into heaven and his session at the right hand of the Father, with his glorious and fearful *coming again*, *have set* before thee thine own gifts from thine own creation

He also left us *as a memorial of his saving passion what we here set forth according to his commandment.* For when he was about *to go forth to his voluntary and ever-memorable and lifegiving* death, taking bread *into his most pure and holy hands and showing it to thee, O God and Father, and giving thanks and* blessing, hallowing, and breaking it, he *gave* it to his holy disciples and apostles, saying, "Take eat: this is my body, which is broken for you for the remission of sins." In the same way, *taking* the cup *of the fruit of the vine*, and mingling it, giving thanks, and blessing and hallowing it, he gave it to *his holy disciples and apostles*, saying, "Drink this, all of you: this is my blood of the new covenant, which is poured out for you and for many for the remission of sins. Do this in remembrance of me: for whenever you eat this bread and drink this cup, you proclaim my death *and confess my resurrection.*"

Therefore, O Master, we also, remembering his *saving* passion *and his lifegiving cross, his three days' burial* and his resurrection from the dead, and his ascension into heaven and his session at *thy* right hand, *God and* Father, with his glorious and fearful *appearing, bringing* before thee thine own gifts from thine own creation in *all and through all:*

> *we praise thee, bless thee, give thanks to thee, O Lord, and pray to thee, our God:*

Epiclesis and Supplication

And we, thy sinful and unworthy servants, pray to thee and we worship thee,

that thou wouldst be graciously pleased that thy Holy Spirit may come upon us and upon these gifts here set forth to hallow and reveal them as the holy of holies;

and make us worthy to partake *of these holy things* for sanctification of soul and body, that we may become one body and one Spirit

and find a share with all thy saints who have found favor with thee since the world began.

[*See list at the conclusion of the intercessions.*]

[*See later petition in this text.*]

Again, remember, Lord, thy one holy catholic and apostolic church and give it peace, for thou hast purchased it with the precious blood of thy Christ. And [remember] all orthodox bishops in it.

Epiclesis and Initial Supplications

Therefore, most holy Master, since thou hast accounted us worthy, sinful and unworthy servants though we are, *to serve at thy holy altar, not because of our own righteousness, for we have done no good thing upon earth, but because of thy mercy and compassion with which thou hast plenteously showered us we dare to draw near to thy holy altar, and, presenting to thee the figures of the holy body and blood of thy Christ, to call upon thee and beseech thee, O thou* Holy One of the holy ones, that thou wouldst be graciously pleased that thy Holy Spirit may come upon us and upon these gifts here set forth to *bless,* hallow, and reveal *this bread as indeed the precious body of thy Christ and this cup as indeed the precious blood of our Lord and God and savior Jesus Christ, shed for the life of the world, and to unite us all, as many as are* partakers *of the one bread and cup, with each other in the communion of the* one *Holy* Spirit: *to allow none of us to partake of the holy body and blood of thy Christ unto judgment or condemnation, but that we may* find *in this way mercy and grace,* with all thy saints who have been pleasing to thee since the world began, our forefathers and fathers, patriarchs, prophets, apostles, preachers, evangelists, martyrs, confessors, doctors, and with all the spirits of the righteous made perfect in faith, especially our most holy, pure, blessed, and glorious lady, the ever-virgin Mary, bearer of God, with the holy John, the forerunner and baptist, with the most renowned, holy, and glorious apostles, with holy N., whose memory we keep, and with all thy saints, at whose prayers, O God, visit us

And remember all those who have fallen asleep in the hope of the resurrection to eternal life: and grant them rest where the light of thy countenance watches over them.

Again *we pray,* remember, Lord, thy holy catholic and apostolic church, *which stretches from one end of the world to the other,* and give it peace, for thou hast purchased it with the precious blood of thy Christ; *and establish this holy house to the consummation of the ages....*

Alexandrian Basil: Supplication continued

Note: The rest of the intercessions in the Byzantine anaphora, not given here, are much expanded. The commemoration of the saints and of the departed, which come at the end of the Alexandrian anaphora, come at the beginning of the Byzantine recension, as can be seen above. There are also other changes in the sequence.

Remember first of all thy servant N., archbishop, and his colleague in the ministry the holy bishop, N., and all who with them rightly divide the word of truth: Grant that they may shepherd thy holy churches, thy flocks, in peace.

Remember, Lord, the presbyterate and the whole diaconate and those who assist and all those in virginity and chastity and all the faithful laity: to have mercy upon them all.

Remember, Lord, this place and those who dwell here in the faith of God.

And remember, Lord, favorable seasons and the fruits of the earth.

And remember those who offer thee these gifts and those for whom they offered them: and grant them a heavenly reward.

Since, Master, it is the command of thine only Son that we share in the commemoration of thy saints, graciously remember also those who have been well-pleasing to thee from the creation of the world, our fathers, patriarchs, prophets, apostles, martyrs, confessors, preachers, evangelists, and all the righteous who have been perfected in the faith, especially the holy and glorious bearer of God, the ever-virgin Mary: through her prayers have mercy upon us and save us for the sake of thy holy name which has been invoked upon us.

Remember likewise all in the priesthood who are now at rest and all from the order of the laity and grant them rest in the bosom of Abraham, Isaac, and Jacob in green pastures by the waters of rest, from which grief, sorrow, and sighing have fled away. [*Names are recited.*] Grant them rest in thy presence.

Preserve in thy faith those of us who dwell here; guide us in thy kingdom; and graciously grant us thy peace at all times:

through Jesus Christ and the Holy Spirit: the Father in the Son, the Son in the Father with the Holy Spirit in the one holy catholic and apostolic church.

An examination of these two recensions of the anaphora demonstrate how a eucharistic prayer can be revised to incorporate new theological concerns and emphases while the basic structure is retained. The much expanded use of biblical citations in the Byzantine version of St. Basil is characteristic of later recensions of eucharistic prayers. Note first of all the preface. The original preface focused on the praise of God (the Father), a traditional theme for the opening of the eucharistic prayer. Theological conflict over the doctrine of the Trinity toward the end of the fourth century led Basil to enrich and recast this material so that its theme shifted to the praise of the triune God, focusing in turn on the Father, the Son, and the Spirit. The Urtext of the anaphora of the apostles also underwent a trinitarian revision, as we have noted, but the redactor of that anaphora simply added the names of the three *personae* in appropriate places; Basil reworked the material much more profoundly.

In a similar way he enriched the account God's economy—creation, the fall, and the redemptive deeds of both the old covenant and the new—vastly expanding the narrative while retaining its basic shape. The institution narrative has been expanded and reworked as well. This narrative has undergone continual revision in liturgical tradition, sometimes being conformed more closely to one biblical account or another, and sometimes being embellished. The anamnesis has been expanded as well, with elaboration of the passion of Christ to include his death and burial. The Byzantine recension has also added an acclamation—a characteristic embellishment at the end of the fourth century. The penitential acclamation in the anaphora of James (see chapter 2) is probably original to that text. But the memorial acclamation of that anaphora and the doxological acclamation which is found in both the anaphora of the apostles and the Byzantine anaphora of Basil distort the flow and syntax of the prayers. The addition of the cue words and the doxological acclamation strain the syntax of both the anaphora of the St. John Chrysostom and the Byzantine recension of the anaphora of St. Basil. They originally belong to a doxological clause, but they are attached to an oblationary clause in these two anaphoras, causing the main verb of the clause to be turned into a participle and straining the syntax.

The Alexandrian anaphora of St. Basil has an epiclesis with what was by the end of the fourth century an archaic theology: the Spirit is invoked on both the gifts and the communicants, but the concern is with the sanctification of the communicants. The Spirit is invoked upon the gifts in order that they may become the means of the sanctification of the communicants—holy things for holy people. By the end of the century, concern had shifted to the consecration of the elements as the body and blood of Christ. Basil's revision of the text makes this plain: the phrase "holy [things] for holy [people]" is replaced as the object of the verb "manifest" with the terms "body and blood" and redeployed as a vocative in address to God: "Holy [One] of the holy [ones]." In addition, the gifts which have been offered are described as the antitypes or figures of Christ's body and blood. The text has also been clericalized: it is no longer the worshippers who are described as "sinful and unworthy servants;" it is now the clergy, who give thanks that God has accounted them worthy to minister.

The expansion of the intercessions of the supplication is a characteristic activity of later redactors of anaphoras. The intercessions are adapted to current needs. The reversal in sequence seems to have been the result of an attempt to make the sequence flow more smoothly: the commemoration of the saints and the departed has been shifted to the first mention of the saints at the conclusion of the epiclesis.

THE FINAL FORM OF THE ANAPHORA OF ST. JAMES

In chapter 2 we examined the probable early form of the anaphora of St. James, the native rite of Jerusalem, working with the description given by Cyril in his baptismal homilies. It is likely that by the end of the century this early anaphora seemed theologically inadequate, lacking as it did a narrative of the economy of salvation and an institution narrative and anamnesis. John Fenwick believes that the redactor of the final form of the anaphora worked with the Alexandrian form of the anaphora of St. Basil to supply what was lacking in his anaphora. He worked with such skill that he produced perhaps the most elegant and logically constructed of the Antiochene anaphoras.[13]

Let us now look at the final text of that anaphora. The text below is a translation of the Syriac form (omitting a section of the anamnesis which is lacking in the Greek), which appears to be earlier than the Greek recension that has come down to us. The bold-faced text is what we isolated in the last chapter as the earlier form of the anaphora before it was reworked (with later embellishments in italics). The added sections appear in ordinary typeface.

It is truly fitting and right, suitable and profitable, to praise thee, to bless thee, to worship thee, to glorify thee, to give thanks to thee, the creator of all creation, visible and invisible. Thou art hymned by the heaven of heavens and all their powers, by the sun and moon and all the choir of stars, by earth, sea, and all that is in them; by the heavenly Jerusalem, the church of the first-born written in heaven, by angels, archangels, thrones, dominions, principalities and powers, and awesome virtues. The cherubim with many eyes and seraphim with six wings, who cover their own faces with two wings and their feet with two and fly with two, cry aloud to one another with unwearying mouths and never silent hymns of praise and with clear voice the triumphal hymn of thy magnificent glory, proclaiming, praising, crying, and saying:

> **Holy, holy, holy, Lord God of Sabaoth. Heaven and earth are full of thy glory. Hosanna in the highest. Blessed is the one that has come and comes in the name of the Lord. Hosanna in the highest.**

Holy art thou, King of the ages and Giver of all holiness; holy too is thine only Son, our Lord and God Jesus Christ; and holy too is thy Holy Spirit, who searches out all things, even thy depths, O God and Father. Holy art thou, almighty, all-powerful, awesome, good, with sympathy especially for that which thou hast fashioned.

Thou didst make man from the earth and grant him the enjoyment of paradise; and when he transgressed thy commandment and fell, thou didst not despise him or abandon him, for thou art good, but thou didst instruct him as a kindly father; thou didst call him through the law; thou didst teach him through the prophets.

Lastly thou didst send thine only Son our Lord and God Jesus Christ into the world to renew thine image. He came down and was made flesh of the Holy Spirit and Mary, the holy virgin bearer of God. He dwelt among humans and ordered all things for the salvation of our race.

When he was about to endure his voluntary death, the sinless for us sinners, in the night when he was handed over for the life and salvation of the world, he took bread in his holy, undefiled, blameless hands, showed it to thee, his God and Father; he gave thanks, blessed, hallowed, and broke it, and gave it to his disciples and apostles, saying, "Take, eat: this is my body, which is broken and distributed for you for the forgiveness of sins."

Likewise after supper he mingled the cup of wine and water, blessed and hallowed it, and gave it to his disciples and apostles, saying, "Drink of this, all of you: this is my blood of the new covenant, which is shed and distributed for you and for many for the forgiveness of sins. Do this in remembrance of me, for as often as you eat this bread and drink this cup, you proclaim the death of the Son of Man and confess his resurrection until he comes."

We proclaim thy death, O Lord, and we confess thy resurrection.

Remembering therefore thy death and resurrection from the dead on the third day and thy return to heaven and thy session at the right hand of thy God and Father and thy glorious and awesome second coming, when thou wilt judge the living and the dead, when thou wilt reward all according to their works: **We therefore offer thee this awesome and bloodless sacrifice, that thou wouldst not deal with us according to our sins nor reward us according to our iniquities, but according to thy loving kindness and love for humankind wouldst blot out the sins of thy suppliants, for thy people and thy church entreats thee:**

Have mercy upon us, almighty Father.

Have mercy upon us, God the Father almighty, and send out upon us and upon these gifts set before thee thy Holy Spirit, *the Lord and giver of life, who with thee and thy Son is enthroned and reigns, consubstantial and coeternal, who spoke by the law and the prophets and in thy new covenant, who descended in the likeness of a dove upon our Lord Jesus Christ at the river Jordan, who descended upon thy holy apostles in the likeness of fiery tongues,* **that he may descend upon them, and make this bread the holy body of Christ and this cup the precious blood of Christ, that they may avail to all who partake of them for sanctification of souls and bodies, for strengthening thy holy catholic church, which thou didst found upon the rock of faith, that the gates of hell should not prevail against it, rescuing it from every heresy, and from the stumbling blocks of those who work lawlessness until the consummation of the age.**

We offer to thee for...[*Extensive intercessions and a doxology conclude the prayer.*]

The added material includes a post-Sanctus, the institution narrative, and the anamnesis. The redactor has apparently worked from the outline of the Alexandrian anaphora of Basil, but developed the material in his own way. He begins with a brief trinitarian development of the threefold "holy" of the Sanctus and continues with the account of the economy of salvation, following rather closely the sequence of Basil's post-Sanctus as far as the account of the incarnation. But unlike Basil, he ends the narrative of Basil's post-Sanctus at this point and inserts the account of the institution in its proper place in the chronological sequence, effectively incorporating it into the narrative. The anamnesis then picks up the sequence once again, expanding the list of events in Basil's anamnesis with material from the remainder of the post-Sanctus. The narrative in the final version of this anaphora thus flows without interruption from creation to the parousia. The redactor ends the anamnesis before Basil's oblation, picking up with the original material from the Jerusalem anaphora which served to introduce the epiclesis.

The result is an anaphoral sequence which begins with the praise of God as creator in the Preface, pre-Sanctus, and Sanctus, continues (after a doxological acknowledgement of the Trinity) with the remembrance of the Son in the post-Sanctus, institution narrative, anamnesis and oblation, and then moves on to the invocation of the Spirit in the epiclesis and the concluding intercessions. It is this structure, a kind of doxological creed, which commended itself so strongly to the Non-Jurors and others after the Reformation.

THE EVOLVING STRUCTURE OF THE WEST SYRIAN ANAPHORAS

The provenance of all the anaphoras considered in chapters 2 and 3 (except that of the *Apostolic Tradition*) is what is sometimes known as greater Syria—that is, what we would call Asia Minor and the Middle East. All of the anaphoras were originally composed in Greek, although the most ancient extant witness to some of them is a translation into another language (Syriac, except for the Alexandrian recension of the anaphora of St. Basil, whose earliest witness is the Sahidic translation). The nucleus of the anaphora of the apostles (the Urtext behind the anaphoras of the Twelve Apostles and St. John Chrysostom) is Antiochene in origin; the nucleus of the anaphora of Basil is Cappadocian; and the nucleus of the anaphora of St. James is Palestinian. These Greek prayers are carefully constructed compositions, with the material fashioned into a single, well-ordered whole. The eucharistic prayers which originated in the Syriac-speaking churches of the region, on the other hand, stayed much closer to the conventions of Jewish euchology, and are best understood as a series of *berakoth,* like those found in the *Didache.*

The work of discovering the nucleus of each of these prayers before they were reworked in the course of the fourth century is of necessity hypothetical: only in the case of the anaphora of St. James do we have reliable external evidence. But it would appear that the nucleus in each case is as follows:

ST. JAMES	THE APOSTLES	ST. BASIL
Preface: Creation's Praise	Preface: God's economy	Preface: Praise of God
Pre-Sanctus		
Sanctus		
		Narrative: God's economy
Oblation/Epiclesis/ Supplication		
	Oblation/Epiclesis/Supplication	Epiclesis/Supplication

The thematic structure of all these anaphoras in general terms is the same: they begin with praise and thanksgiving and move on to supplication. The supplication always begins with a petition for the church (sometimes together with a preceding petition for the communicants). But each anaphora has its distinctive form of praise or thanksgiving. In St. James the preface opens with the praise of creation, which flows quite naturally into the Sanctus. In this case the Sanctus is an integral part of the anaphora. In the case of the anaphora of the apostles, the original nucleus seems to be a very succinct account of the divine economy in the preface and continues, it would appear, with the oblation which introduces the supplication. As for St. Basil, it is difficult to be sure what shape the original nucleus took. The most carefully constructed unit in this prayer is the narrative of God's economy in what is now the post-Sanctus. The pre-Sanctus and Sanctus do not appear to be integral to the prayer, nor do the institution narrative and anamnesis. It is difficult to know what to make of the preface (there is a lacuna in the Sahidic text of the anaphora, and the surviving text only begins at the end of the preface). It would appear that the original nucleus might have included the praise of God in the preface, the narrative which now forms the post-Sanctus, the epiclesis with its oblation and the supplication.

The nucleus of the anaphora of St. James provided a model for incorporating the Sanctus, and the eucharistic prayer of the *Apostolic Tradition* provided a model of a carefully structured prayer which served as an incentive for further revision of the older eucharistic prayers in this region. Here then are the origins of the elements added to the primitive nucleus of the anaphora in the region:

> Pre-Sanctus, Sanctus (and epicletic embolism on the Sanctus): Jerusalem
> Post-Sanctus Narrative: preface of the *Apostolic Tradition*
> Institution narrative as a part of the thanksgiving: *Apostolic Tradition*
> Anamnesis joined to the institution narrative: *Apostolic Tradition*
> Epiclesis: St. James and *Apostolic Tradition*

The characteristic shape of these anaphoras is a first thanksgiving concluding with the Sanctus, a second thanksgiving linked to the first by the word "holy" and concluding with the institution narrative and anamnesis, and a supplication beginning with an invocation of the Spirit. In their final form, these prayers have acquired one or more acclamations. It is the careful integration of new material in a well-ordered sequence that distinguishes this tradition from Alexandria, where new elements were simply appended to the original nucleus of the anaphora of St. Mark, and from Rome, where the Sanctus concludes the thanksgiving and the institution narrative and anamnesis are part of the supplication.

THE THEOLOGY OF THE WEST SYRIAN ANAPHORAS

Early eucharistic prayers took the form of thanksgiving and supplication over the bread and wine, which the church understood as the fulfilment of its Lord's command to do this in his remembrance. The thanksgiving and the elements over which it was said were understood as the church's sacrifice of praise and thanksgiving. The church understood the elements to be consecrated for the purposes of communion in the body and blood of Christ by the thanksgiving said over them.

The New Testament itself understands the church's worship as a proleptic participation in the worship of heaven. This understanding led to the incorporation of the Sanctus into the eucharistic prayer so that the church on earth might join in the angelic praise of God. The letter to the Hebrews also understood the heavenly altar to be the place where Christ pleaded his sacrifice before the throne of grace, and the church came to think of its sacrifice of praise and thanksgiving as united to Christ's pleading of his sacrifice at the heavenly altar. By the end of the fourth century, the importance of the Sanctus as a constituent element of the church's participation in the heavenly liturgy was recessive, and the understanding of the bread and wine as antitypes of the sacrifice of Christ presented in the heavenly liturgy predominated. This identification of the church's sacrifice with Christ's own sacrifice (which finds its most explicit articulation in the anaphoras of the apostles and of St. James) led to a propitiatory understanding of what was originally conceived as a sacrifice of praise and thanksgiving.

The institution narrative entered the eucharistic prayer as the warrant for the celebration of the eucharist, along with the anamnesis as the church's pledge to fulfill Christ's command. But once it had entered the prayer, it tended to assume much greater importance. This can be seen by the "manual acts" which it has attracted to itself in almost all traditions. Although the predominant theology of consecration in the West Syrian tradition came to attribute "consecration" and "transformation" of the bread and wine to the epiclesis, we can also find commentators— the most notable of whom is John Chrysostom—who ascribe this role to the words of Christ in the institution narrative. This tendency can also be seen in the Amens which attached themselves to the words of Christ and to the rubrication which stipulates that they be said aloud. This theology of consecration was to have a long future. Such an interpretation, however, is seldom justified by either the text or the structure of a eucharistic prayer.

NOTES

[1] See the discussion of church orders in Paul F. Bradshaw, *The Search for the Origins of Christian Worship: Sources and Methods for the Study of Early Liturgy* (New York: Oxford, 1992), chapter 4.

[2] The text may be found in Brightman, *Liturgies Eastern and Western*, pages 228-234. Recent scholars who treat this anaphora as an historical curiosity which never came into actual use have generally ignored the Ethiopian anaphora.

[3] My translation from the Latin text given in Gregory Dix and Henry Chadwick, *The Apostolic Tradition of St. Hippolytus of Rome, Bishop and Martyr* (Ridgefield, Conn.: Morehouse Publishing, 1992). The principal difficult for translators is the epiclesis, whose syntax is awkward. It may be that the original reading was "grant to all who partake of these holy things."

[4] See the analysis in Mazza, *The Origins of the Eucharistic Prayer*, chapter 4. Mazza believes that Hippolytus has drawn on the literature of paschal homilies in constructing the narrative of the two strophes of thanksgiving.

[5] The *Apostolic Tradition* is the basic source for book 8 of the *Apostolic Constitutions*, which is a compilation of Antiochene provenance. This fact serves to demonstrate a knowledge of the *Apostolic Tradition* in the region, so that it served as a model for the incorporation of institution narrative, anamnesis, and epiclesis in a eucharistic prayer. The basic structural outline for West Syria is obtained by prefacing material on the praise of God or on creation and the Sanctus to the elements found in the *Apostolic Tradition*.

[6] See the introduction to the texts from book 8 of the *Apostolic Constitutions* in Jasper and Cuming, *Prayers of the Eucharist*, page 103, and Enrico Mazza, *The Origins of the Eucharistic Prayer*, pages 129-134, for use of material from the *Apostolic Tradition* in the eucharistic prayer of book 8.

[7] See Geoffrey Cuming, "Four Very Early Anaphoras," in *Worship* 58 (1984), pages 168-172, and "The Shape of the Anaphora," in *Studia Patristica* 20 (1989), pages 333-345), and John Fenwick, *Fourth Century Anaphoral Construction Techniques* (Bramcote, Notts.: Grove, 1986) and *'The Missing Oblation': The Contents of the Early Antiochene Anaphora* (Bramcote, Notts.: Grove, 1989).

[8] Some scholars believe that not all early texts included a supplication. It is also possible that the Sanctus may have been an original component of some texts. See the studies cited in note 6.

[9] The text of John Chrysostom is translated from the Greek text of Brightman, *Liturgies Eastern and Western*, pages 321-327, which reproduces the earliest text extant, that of the Barberini MS 336. This presents the Italian recension. Later manuscripts of the Constantinopolitan recension vary slightly, primarily in the intercessions, where they probably preserve an earlier text. For the Twelve Apostles, see the French translation of the Syriac text printed in G. Khouri-Sarkis, "L'origine syrienne de l'anaphore byzantine de S. Jean Chrysostome," in *L'Orient syrien* 7 (1962), pages 3-68. English translations of both anaphoras may be found in Jasper and Cuming, *Prayers of the Eucharist*, pages 124-134.

[10] This issue is addressed by John Fenwick in *'The Missing Oblation': The Contents of the Early Antiochene Anaphora*, and Robert Taft in "Reconstituting the Oblation of the Chrysostom Anaphora: An Exercise in Comparative Liturgy," in *Orientalia Christiana Periodica* 59 (1993), pages 387-402. I have come to somewhat different conclusions from either of these authors.

[11] *Das eucharistische Hochgebet der Basileiosliturgie. Textgeschichtliche Untersuchungen und kritische Ausgabe* (Münster, 1931).

[12] Fenwick, *The Anaphoras of St. Basil and St. James.* The translations of the Alexandrian recension of Basil in this chapter are based on his text, while those for the Byzantine form are based on the text in Brightman, *Liturgies Eastern and Western,* pages 321-337. English translations of the two versions may be found in Jasper and Cuming, *Prayers of the Eucharist: Early and Reformed*, pages 70-72 and 116-123.

[13] The text here is based on the Latin translation of the Syriac text is printed in John Fenwick, *The Anaphoras of St. Basil and St. James*, who prints it in parallel with the (longer) Greek text. An English translation of the text of St. James (with the additional material of the Greek text indicated as bracketed material) may be found in Jasper and Cuming, *Prayers of the Eucharist: Early and Reformed*, pages 90-99. I have omitted the second invocation of the Holy Spirit in the epiclesis, which is not found in the Greek text and is probably a later accretion. I have also omitted the doxological acclamation which appears to have been taken over from the anaphora of the Twelve Apostles into the Syriac text and interrupts the flow of the prayer.

CHAPTER FOUR

THE EUCHARISTIC SACRIFICE
ALEXANDRIA AND ROME

✦ ✦ ✦ ✦ ✦ ✦ ✦ ✦ ✦ ✦ ✦ ✦ ✦

I n the evolution of the liturgy both the Sanctus and the institution narrative (coupled with the anamnesis) represent additions to the primitive structure of the eucharistic prayer. Recent research appears to suggest that neither was present in the primitive texts which lie behind what we know as the Alexandrian anaphora of St. Mark and the Roman Canon. The liturgical traditions of these two sees were originally closely interrelated. Many scholars have noted the textual and thematic similarities between particular portions of these two eucharistic prayers. But in their present state these two prayers show little apparent structural similarity. How are we to account for these facts?

Enrico Mazza has set about to explain how these texts evolved so differently.[1] A key factor in resolving the puzzle is the discovery of a very early text of the anaphora of St. Mark known as the Strasbourg papyrus. The papyrus apparently dates between 300 and 500 C.E.; the text is very early and was probably expanded in the fourth century. When the papyrus was first discovered in 1928 many assumed it was a fragment of the full anaphora. But the presence of a doxology at the conclusion of the intercessions suggests that it presents us with the full text of the early form of the anaphora.[2]

This suggestion proved astounding to many, for the text consists of two strophes of what we would ordinarily classify as the preface of a eucharistic prayer and a set of intercessions. There are *lacunae* in the text—the first part of the preface and a good portion of the intercessions. This makes it difficult for us to know what the original scope of the intercessions was, for those in the final form of the anaphora of St. Mark have been greatly expanded. But all the parts of the anaphora which have textual or thematic parallels in the Roman canon are found in the part of the final text of the anaphora which precedes the Sanctus. What this suggests is that the primitive form of both eucharistic prayers consisted of a preface (consisting of two strophes of thanksgiving) and a supplication (the intercessions), and that other parts of the prayer in the two traditions are later additions. What has caused the present structural dissimilarity is the way in which these additions were made. In the Roman canon, the Sanctus was placed after the two strophes of thanksgiving and the institution narrative, with the anamnesis inserted into the supplication. In the anaphora of St. Mark, additional material was simply added on to the original text in two blocks—first the introduction to the Sanctus, the Sanctus, and its epiclesis; then the institution narrative, the anamnesis, and the second epiclesis. If we remove these additions in each tradition, the parallels immediately stand out clearly.[3]

THE EVOLUTION OF THE ANAPHORA OF ST. MARK

Let us look at the texts in each of the two traditions in turn, and then see how the early forms of each compare. We begin with the earliest form of the anaphora of St. Mark as it is found in the Strasbourg papyrus. The translation below includes the first two strophes, the opening intercession of the supplication (the prayer for the church), and the final doxology. I have not attempted to reconstruct the full missing portion of the first strophe or the intercessions which follow that for the church. The italicized beginning of the first strophe is borrowed from the later anaphora of St. Mark to put the text of the Strasbourg papyrus in context.

> *It is truly fitting and right*...to bless thee night and day: thou who madest heaven and all that is in it, the earth and what is on earth, seas and rivers and all that is in them; who madest humankind *after* thine own image and likeness. Thou madest everything through thy wisdom, through the true light, thy Son our Lord Jesus Christ. Giving thanks through him to thee with him and the Holy Spirit, we offer the reasonable sacrifice, this unbloodly worship which all

> nations offer to thee "from the rising of the sun to its setting," from north to south, for thy "name is great among all the nations, and in every place incense is offered to thy holy name and a pure sacrifice." Over this sacrifice and offering we pray and beseech thee: remember thy one holy catholic church, all thy peoples and all thy flocks. Provide the peace which is from heaven in all our hearts and grant us also the peace of this life...through our Lord; through whom be glory to thee for ever and ever.[4]

The first strophe of this text focuses on praise for creation and shows marked similarities to the *Yotzer*, cited in chapter 2: note the allusion to Psalm 104:24 and Isaiah 45:7, both given a Christological interpretation here: creation is through Christ as the wisdom of God and the true light is none other than Jesus Christ. The second strophe designates the thanksgiving as the offering by the couplet "giving thanks...we offer" and then cites the pure sacrifice of Malachi 1:11, which functions as the warrant or institution for the rite. The opening of the third strophe is the prayer for the church—which figures in some way in almost all early eucharistic prayers as the primary intercession of the supplication.

To this original nucleus, two further blocks of material came to be added in the course of time to form the anaphora of St. Mark as we know it. These additions had been made by the sixth century, for we find a fragmentary text beginning with the epiclesis from the first block in a sixth-century Greek parchment in the John Rylands Library in Manchester and in an eighth-century Coptic wooden tablet in the British Museum. The first block consists of an introduction, the Sanctus (in Egyptian form, without the Benedictus qui venit), and an epiclesis or invocation, linked to the Sanctus in the Alexandrian tradition by the key words "full" in the Sanctus and "full" and "fill" in the epiclesis. This is the text as we find it in the two early witnesses, supplemented by the introduction and the Sanctus from the Coptic version of the final form of the text.

> *After a bidding from the deacon, the celebrant continues:*
>
> For "thou art above all rule and authority and power and dominion and above every name that is named, not only in this age but in that which is to come." Beside thee stand thousands of thousands and ten thousands of ten thousands of angels and archangels. Beside thee stand thy two most honorable living creatures, the cherubim with many eyes and the seraphim with six wings, who cover their faces with two wings and their feet with two and fly with two. Everything at all times hallows thee, but with all that hallow thee thou dost receive also, Lord and Master, our hallowing, as with them we hymn thee and say:

> Holy, holy, holy, Lord of Sabaoth. Heaven and earth are full of thy glory.
>
> Full in truth are heaven and earth of thy glory through our Lord and Savior Jesus Christ: fill, O God, this sacrifice also with thy blessing through thy Holy Spirit.[5]

We have already seen how important the Sanctus was in the anaphoras on which Cyril of Alexandria and Theodore of Mopsuestia commented in their baptismal homilies. In those anaphoras the Sanctus was integral to the structure of the eucharistic prayer. Theologically it served to legitimate the Christian eucharist as the church's participation in the worship of heaven. The Sanctus also appears at a very early stage of development in the Alexandrian tradition (appearing in local usages such as those of Sarapion as well as the Alexandrian anaphoras of St. Basil and St. Mark), but it does not appear integral to the structure of these prayers to the same extent as it did in some of the early Syrian anaphoras. Apart from the Alexandrian anaphora of St. Basil, it is always closely linked with the form of epiclesis noted above—an epiclesis which grounds the consecration of the elements in the church's participation in the liturgy of heaven.

This block is followed by a second one, consisting of the institution narrative, the anamnesis, and a second epiclesis. The text as it is found in two early witnesses is as follows. The final part of the last paragraph (the result clause and doxology) is difficult to read in the Rylands manuscript and lacking in the British Museum tablet, so I have completed it from the Coptic version of the final form of the anaphora.

> For our Lord and Savior and King of all, Jesus Christ, in the night when he was betrayed and willingly underwent death, took bread in his holy and undefiled and blessed hands, looked up to heaven to thee, the Father of all, blessed, gave thanks over it, sanctified, broke, and gave it to his disciples and apostles, saying, "Take and eat of this, all of you: this is my body, which is given for you for the forgiveness of your sins, Do this in remembrance of me."
>
> Likewise, after supper, he took a cup, blessed, sanctified, and gave it to them, saying, "Take this and drink from it, all of you; this is my blood of the new covenant, which is shed for many for the forgiveness of their sins. Do this in remembrance of me. For as often as you eat this bread and drink this cup, you proclaim my death and confess my resurrection."
>
> Proclaiming, therefore, the death of thine only-begotten Son, our Lord and Savior Jesus Christ, and confessing his resurrection and his ascension into heaven, and looking for his glorious coming, we have set before thee these gifts from thine own, this bread and this cup.

> We pray and beseech thee to send thy Holy Spirit and thy power
> upon these [gifts] set before thee, on this bread and this cup, and to
> make the bread the body of Christ and the cup the blood of the new
> covenant of our Lord and Savior Jesus Christ, that they may avail
> to all of us who receive for faith, for sobriety, for healing, for
> renewal of soul, body, and spirit, for fellowship in eternal life and
> immortality, that in this as in everything thy all-holy and honorable
> and glorious name may be glorified and praised and sanctified, with
> Jesus Christ and the Holy Spirit.[6]

This block of material shows the influence of the tradition represented by the anaphora of St. James. Particularly noteworthy is the conclusion of the institution narrative, which adds a citation of 1 Corinthians 11:26, changed here from the third to the first person, so that it
becomes part of the warrant given by Christ. This then becomes the
basis of the anamnesis: a characteristic of the anaphora of St. James and
related texts, which differentiates them from those which start from the
command, "Do this in remembrance of me." The epiclesis in the early
form of the text of St. Mark is much simpler than what is found in St.
James; the final text has been elaborated considerably and resembles St.
James much more closely.

THE EVOLUTION OF THE ROMAN CANON

The structure of the anaphora of St. Mark consists of an opening
strophe of praise and thanksgiving for creation, a second strophe of
thanksgiving which offers the eucharist as a sacrifice, and the supplication. Unlike Eastern liturgical traditions, where the entire text of an
anaphora is fixed, Latin traditions incorporate variable texts in their
eucharistic prayers. The most important of the variable texts in the
Roman canon is the preface. In its final form the Roman canon had a
very limited number of proper prefaces, but the earliest collection of
eucharistic propers, the so-called sacramentary of Verona, had a preface
for every proper—257 in all! The oldest of these prefaces, which probably date to the fourth and fifth centuries, appear to antedate the incorporation of the Sanctus into the Roman canon, for thematically they do not
lead into the text of the Sanctus. Most frequently they end with a simple
"per" (through), an indication that they probably continued "per Chris-
tum dominum nostrum, per quem petimus et precamur...": that is, they
led into the beginning of the intercessions of the canon, which now begins
"Te igitur." It is characteristic of these prefaces that they consist of a first
strophe of thanksgiving and a second strophe which designates the
eucharist as the offering of the sacrifice of praise. The second strophe

couples such words and phrases as "gratiarum actiones," "laetantes," "recolentes," "celebrantes," and "venerantes" with verbs of offering and terms for the sacrifice, most commonly "hostias laudis"—the Latin equivalent of the Greek words coupled in St. Mark—"giving thanks …we offer." In its earlier form the Roman canon moved directly from the two strophes of the preface into the prayer for the church in the supplication.

We can see this structure clearly in the preface which the sacramentary of Verona gives for the vigil of Pentecost. By the time of the Gelasian sacramentary this preface retained its two original strophes and indicated a third, leading into the Sanctus; in its final form, it lost the second strophe and acquired a somewhat different introduction to the Sanctus. In the process the structural shape of the early form of the preface was lost. Here are the three versions in parallel columns:[7]

It is truly meet and right, fitting and salutary, that we should at all times and in all places give thanks unto thee, O Lord, holy Father, almighty, everlasting God through Christ our Lord: Who, ascending into heaven and sitting at thy right hand, poured forth the promised Holy Spirit on thy adopted children.	It is truly meet and right, fitting and salutary, that we should at all times and in all places give thanks unto thee, O Lord, holy Father, almighty, everlasting God through Christ our Lord: Who, ascending into heaven and sitting at thy right hand, poured forth the promised Holy Spirit on thy adopted children.	It is truly meet and right, fitting and salutary, that we should at all times and in all places give thanks unto thee, O Lord, holy Father, almighty, everlasting God through Christ our Lord: Who, ascending into heaven and sitting at thy right hand, poured forth the promised Holy Spirit on thy adopted children.
Rejoicing, therefore, at thy altars, O Lord of hosts, we offer to thee sacrifices of praise, etc. [through Christ our Lord:]	Rejoicing, therefore, at thy altars, O Lord of hosts, we offer to thee sacrifices of praise through Christ our Lord:	
[through whom we beg and beseech thee…And we pray thee, that thou wouldst send thy Holy Spirit upon these gifts here set forth…	whom [the angels] praise… "Holy, holy, holy …"]	through whom the angels… "Holy, holy, holy …"

The oldest witness to the Roman canon as we know it is found in the baptismal homilies of Ambrose of Milan at the end of the fourth century. Similar testimony is found in a post-Sanctus (labeled as a post-pridie) and a post-pridie in Mozarabic sources. Ambrose gives the actual text only after the second part of the Mozarabic post-Sanctus; for what precedes it we must rely on his general description. In the table below, the first column has the material from Ambrose, the second the material from Mozarabic sources, and the third their later Roman parallels. Section titles are the Latin incipits; the description of the first part of the canon in Ambrose is given in italics:

Ambrose	Mozarabic Sources	Roman Canon
Laus Deo defertur...	[Preface]	[Preface]
Oratio petitur		
pro populo,	Per quem te petimus	Te igitur
pro regibus	[lacking]	[lacking]
pro caeteris	Memorare etiam/	Memento, Domine
Fac nobis	Quorum oblationem	Quam oblationem
Qui pridie	[Institution Narrative]	Qui pridie
Ergo memores	[lacking]	Unde et memores
Et petimus et precamur	Precamur et rogamus	Supra quae/Supplices
[Doxology]	[Doxology]	Per ipsum

The following sections of the Roman canon appear, then, to be additions to the text in Ambrose's time: Communicantes, Hanc oblationem, Memento etiam, Nobis quoque, and Per quem haec omnia. Of these, the Memento etiam (the petition for the departed) and the Nobis quoque have parallels in the anaphora of St. Mark and may be very early.

Let us now look at what appear to be the oldest texts (first column) and compare them with their equivalents in the earliest text of the Roman canon (second column), beginning with the Te igitur. The incipits (in italics) will indicate the source.[8]

MOZARABIC SOURCES/AMBROSE

Per quem te petimu

By whom we beseech and beg thee, almighty Father, that thou wouldst deem accepted and wouldst graciously bless these gifts and these unblemished sacrifices, which we offer to thee first of all for thy holy catholic church spread throughout the world. Graciously grant it peace.

Memorare etiam/Quorum oblationem

Remember also, O Lord, thy servants N. and N., [who pay their vows to thee, the living and true God, in honor of thy saints N. and N.] for the forgiveness of all their sins and graciously account their offering blessed, proper, and spiritual, for it is the image and likeness of the body and blood of Jesus Christ thy Son and our redeemer.

ROMAN CANON

Te igitur

Therefore, most merciful Father, we beg and beseech thee through Jesus Christ thy Son our Lord that thou wouldst deem accepted and wouldst bless these gifts and these holy and unblemished sacrifices, which we offer to thee first of all for thy holy catholic church spread throughout the world. Graciously grant it peace, guard and rule it

Memento, Domine/Quam oblationem

Remember, Lord, thy servants N. and N. and all here present whose faith is known to thee and who offer to thee this sacrifice of praise for themselves and for all their families, for the redemption of their souls, for the hope of salvation and of their safety; [and] they pay their vows to thee, the eternal God, living and true. Do thou, O God, we beseech thee, graciously account this offering in all things blessed, fitting, proper, spiritual, and acceptable: that it may become for us the body and blood of thy beloved son our Lord Jesus Christ.

MOZARABIC SOURCES/AMBROSE

Qui pridie (Ambrose)

Who on the day before he suffered took bread into his holy hands, looked up to heaven to thee, holy Father, almighty, everlasting God, and, giving thanks, blessed it, broke it, and gave it, when broken, to his disciples and apostles, saying, "Take this and eat it, all of you: For this is my body which will be broken for many." In the same way after supper he also took the cup, looked up to heaven to thee, holy Father, almighty everlasting God, and, giving thanks, blessed it and gave it to his apostles and disciples, saying, "Take this and drink from it all of you: For this is my blood. Whenever you do this, you will do it in remembrance of me until I come again."

Ergo memores

Mindful therefore of his most glorious passion and resurrection from the dead and ascension into heaven, we offer to thee this spotless offering, this reasonable offering, this unbloody offering, this holy bread and chalice of eternal life.

Et petimus et precamur

And we beg and pray thee that thou wouldst take this offering to thy altar on high, borne by the hands of thine angels, as thou didst take the gifts of thy servant Abel and the sacrifice of our father Abraham and the offering made by thy high priest Melchizedek.

[Doxology]

ROMAN CANON

Qui pridie

Who on the day before he suffered took bread into his holy and venerable hands and, giving thanks to thee, his almighty Father, with eyes lifted up toward heaven, blessed it, broke it, and gave it to his disciples, saying, "Take this and eat it, all of you: For this is my body." In the same way after supper, taking also this excellent cup into his holy and venerable hands and giving thanks, he blessed it and gave it to his disciples, saying, "Take and drink of this, all of you: For this is the cup of my blood of the new and eternal testament, the mystery of faith, which will be shed for you and for many for the forgiveness of sins. Whenever you do this, do it in remembrance of me."

Unde et memores

[We are] mindful therefore, O Lord, of the blessed passion of Christ thy Son our Lord and his resurrection from the dead and his glorious ascension into heaven, [and] we thy servants and thy holy people offer unto thine excellent majesty, from thine own gifts bestowed on us, a pure offering, a holy offering, a spotless offering, the holy bread of eternal life and the chalice of everlasting salvation.

Supra quae/Supplices

Graciously look upon them with a favorable and serene countenance: and accept them as thou didst graciously accept the gifts of thy servant the righteous Abel and the sacrifice of our father Abraham, and the offering made by thy high priest Melchizedek, a holy sacrifice, a spotless oblation.

We humbly beseech thee, almighty God, to bid these gifts be borne by the hands of thy holy angel to thy altar on high in the sight of thy divine majesty: that as many as shall partake at this altar of the most holy body and blood of thy Son may be filled with every heavenly blessing and grace: through Christ our Lord:

By him and with him and in him, in the unity of the Holy Spirit, all honor and glory be unto thee, O God the Father almighty, for ever and ever. *Amen.*

If we carefully analyze the text of the canon above, which appears to be the earliest form of the text which follows the preface, all of it is supplicatory in character. Even the institution narrative (with the anamnesis which is attached to it) is not an independent paragraph but an embolism or attachment to the Quorum oblationem or Quam oblationem, which is a prayer for the acceptance of the offering.

The Roman canon as we now know it includes several other sections. The Communicantes is a festal embolism to the Memento Domine, attached to it as a participial phrase. The Hanc oblationem which follows is in origin a special addition for specific intentions on special occasions (such as the eucharists of baptismal scrutinies and baptisms, marriages, and ordinations). Two sections which follow the Supplices—the Memento etiam and the Nobis quoque, are not attested in Ambrose or Mozarabic sources, but have close parallels in the intercessions of the anaphora of the Strasbourg papyrus. The Per quem which follows is an embolism to blessings of special offerings (such as the oil of unction) at the eucharist—and so not part of the ordinary text.

A COMPARISON OF THE ALEXANDRIAN TEXTS AND THE ROMAN CANON

All of the portions of the early form of the text of the Roman canon above except the block of material which includes the Quam oblationem, the Qui pridie, and the Unde et memores have parallels in the Strasbourg papyrus or (in the case of the Supra quae/Supplices) in the initial intercessions of the final text of the anaphora of St. Mark. The block which we just noted has certain thematic parallels with the last block of material in the final form of the anaphora of St. Mark, but the two blocks appear to originate in quite different traditions. Let us look at this material in parallel columns:[9]

ROMAN CANON	STRASBOURG PAPYRUS/ST. MARK
Variable Preface	**Fixed Preface (Strasbourg)**
strophe of thanksgiving	strophe of thanksgiving
strophe offering sacrifice of thanksgiving	strophe offering sacrifice of thanksgiving
Per quem te petimus (Te igitur)	**Prayer for the church (Strasbourg)**
By whom we beseech and beg thee, almighty Father, that thou wouldst deem accepted and wouldst graciously bless these gifts and these unblemished sacrifices, which we offer to thee first of all for thy holy catholic church spread throughout the world. Graciously grant it peace.	Over this sacrifice and offering we pray and beseech thee: remember thy one holy catholic church, all thy peoples and all thy flocks. Provide the peace which is from heaven in all our hearts and grant us also the peace of this life....
Et petimus et precamur	**Commendation of offering (St. Mark)**
And we beg and pray thee that thou wouldst take this offering to thy altar on high, borne by the hands of thine angels, as thou didst take the gifts of thy servant Abel and the sacrifice of our father Abraham and the offering made by thy high priest Melchizedek.	Receive, O Lord, the thankofferings of those who offer the sacrifices, much or little, secretly or openly, willing but unable, at your spiritual altar in heaven by the ministry of your archangels, and those who offered the offerings today; as thou didst accept the gifts of thy righteous Abel, the sacrifice of our father Abraham, and the widow's two mites;
Final Clause of Supplices	
that as many as shall partake at this altar of the most holy body and blood of thy Son may be filled with every heavenly blessing and grace: through Christ our Lord:	and give them imperishable things for perishable, heavenly things for earthly, eternal for temporal.
Memento etiam/Nobis quoque	**Prayer for the departed (St. Mark)**
Remember, also, O Lord, thy servants N. and N., who went before us with the sign of faith and now rest in the sleep of peace. To them, O Lord, and to all who rest in Christ, we pray that thou wouldst grant a place of refreshment, light, and peace: through the same Christ our Lord. Amen.	Give rest, to the souls of our fathers and brothers who have fallen asleep, remembering our forefathers from the beginning, the fathers, patriarchs, prophets, apostles, martyrs, confessors, righteous men, every spirit perfected in the faith.... Refresh their souls and count them worthy of the kingdom of heaven;
Graciously grant to us sinners as well, trusting in the multitude of thy mercies, some part and fellowship with thy holy apostles and martyrs...into whose company we pray thee to admit us, reckoning not our merit, but thy forgiveness: through Christ our Lord.	and grant the ends of our lives to be Christian and well-pleasing, and give us to have a part and lot with all your saints.

The structural and thematic relationship of the parallel forms is apparent. Note that the commendation of the offering and the prayer for the departed occur in the reverse sequence in the final form of the anaphora of St. Mark. The prayer for the departed also occurs at the end of the Strasbourg papyrus, but the text there is so fragmentary that it is hard to piece it together. The Alexandrian text of the prayer for the departed is more primitive than the Roman: there is no apparent distinction between the saints and the rest of the departed. The commendation of the offering may have an equivalent at the end of the Strasbourg papyrus, but the fragmentary state of the end of the text makes it difficult to be sure. Ligier proposes the following reading for the last lines of the text: "By their authority accept this prayer at thy heavenly altar...and graciously bestow spiritual gifts upon them."[10]

We should further note that the intercessions of the supplication are the part of the eucharist that underwent the most alteration in the course of time. They were vastly expanded in the final form of the anaphora of St. Mark; the Memento etiam and the Nobis quoque seem to be very early additions to the Roman text and the Communicantes and Hanc igitur are later additions.

The primitive anaphora of St. Mark reached its final form by adding on two blocks of material at the end—first the block of material related to the Sanctus, and then the block of material related to the institution narrative. The Roman canon, on the other hand, inserted these blocks of material at what seemed appropriate places in the original prayer. First the block of material related to the institution narrative was added to the supplication. This block of material is particularly important as the warrant for the rite in the Roman canon, which lacks the citation of Malachi 1:ll which is found as the warrant in the Strasbourg papyrus. Then the Sanctus and its introduction were added at the conclusion of what we now call the preface.

We should take particular note of the block of material related to the institution narrative. The anamnesis is, as almost always, coupled to the narrative. But the narrative itself is attached to a plea for the acceptance and transformation of the offering, joined to it as a relative clause. The ancient form of this first commendation of the offering pleads that it be found acceptable because it is the figure of Christ's body and blood. Like the Sanctus in the anaphora of Cyril, it links the worship of the church on earth to the worship of the church in heaven. But once St. Ambrose had identified the words of Christ as the "words of consecration," this seemed too weak a plea. And so the later Roman canon did not offer them as "figures" (Ambrose) or "image and likeness" (Mozarabic texts), but asked that they *become for us* the body and blood of Christ. Once this had occurred, the institution narrative became the focal point of the entire prayer.

A final feature of the rubrication is important to note. In some early manuscripts, the rubric "Incipit canon actionis" is found before the initial dialogue of the eucharistic prayer. In these manuscripts, the Te igitur follows without a break on the text of the Sanctus: the words do not even begin on a new line. But later in the middle ages, the preface and Sanctus (recited aloud) came to be sharply distinguished from the rest of the prayer (recited silently until the final doxology). The "T" of Te igitur received special treatment, and was often elaborated after the tenth century into a picture of the crucifixion. The rubric which indicated the beginning of the canon was eventually moved to a position just before the Te igitur. The thanksgiving of the eucharistic prayer (the canon actionis), its original core, was thus set off from the prayer and treated as a proem, and the supplication, originally understood as the conclusion of the prayer, was now treated as the whole of the prayer.[11]

A Word about the Gallican and Mozarabic Rites

At a very early stage the rite of Milan, customarily called the Ambrosian rite, adopted the Roman canon. This already appears to be the case at the end of the fourth century, for it is a form of the Roman canon that Ambrose cites, as we have seen, in his baptismal catecheses. Two other traditions in the West—those of Frankish territories (the Gallican rite) and Spain (the Mozarabic rite)—preserved a far greater degree of variability in the eucharistic prayer than any other tradition.[12] The Roman rite had a variable preface and a degree of variability in adaptations of the sections known as Communicantes and Hanc igitur in the final form of the prayer. But in Gaul and Spain the only fixed parts of the prayer were the Sanctus, the institution narrative, and the final doxology. In each of these two traditions (which are in fact two variants of a single tradition) the text between the Sanctus and the institution narrative and between that narrative and the final doxology was variable. This gave the eucharistic prayer in these traditions the following shape:

GALLICAN TRADITION	MOZARABIC TRADITION
Dialogue	Dialogue
Contestatio or Immolatio (Preface)	Illatio (Preface)
Sanctus	Sanctus
Post-Sanctus	Post-Sanctus
Secreta or Mysterium (Institution Narrative)	Secreta (Institution Narrative)
Post-Secreta or Post-Mysterium	Post-Pridie
Doxology	Doxology

This outline gives the impression of structural uniformity in the eucharistic prayer. But this uniformity is illusory because the variable parts of the prayer show wide thematic diversity. These variable parts are at times quite prolix. The prefaces do not reveal the thematic structure of the oldest Roman prefaces, which have one strophe of thanksgiving and a second strophe identifying the rite as a sacrifice of thanksgiving. The post-Sanctus frequently makes use of "holy" as a link with the preface (a characteristic of the West Syrian tradition), but its content varies widely. The variable section after the institution narrative frequently has an epiclesis, but may also incorporate an anamnesis or an oblation. As we have already seen, Roman texts (Memento etiam/Quorum oblationem and a version of Supra quae/Supplices) could be used as a post-Sanctus and post-Pridie in the Mozarabic rite. As in the tradition of Jerusalem, the institution narrative concludes with some variant of 1 Corinthians 11:26. We are dealing here with eclectic liturgical traditions. What is noteworthy is the observable influence in many of the texts of East and West Syrian traditions. This influence can be seen in other liturgical texts as well, and even in the architectural disposition of churches (especially in Spain).

THE THEOLOGY OF THE EUCHARISTIC PRAYER

The early form of the eucharistic prayer in each of the two traditions is a sacrifice of praise and thanksgiving offered to the Father, and the language of sacrifice predominates in the final form of the prayer in each tradition—especially in the Roman canon. This sacrifice is associated in later forms of each prayer with the bread and wine, which themselves are God's gifts bestowed upon us by his bounty and returned to him in an offering of the firstfruits of creation. In each tradition the sacrifice is also understood as propitiatory: in the Strasbourg papyrus, intercession is made "over this sacrifice and offering;" in the Roman canon, the gifts and sacrifices are "offered for" the church." In the later form of the Roman canon God is asked to "remember" those who make the offerings (Memento Domine) and their intentions (Hanc oblationem). Neither prayer explicitly associates the eucharist with the *sacrifice* of Christ, as later eucharistic theology would do. It is the sacrifice of the church, made possible through the gifts which God has bestowed upon us and which we offer back to God. The early forms of the Roman canon come close to such an association when they speak of the gifts offered as the "figure" or the "image and likeness" of Christ's body and blood.

Different theologies of consecration are implicit in the various stages of the evolution of the eucharistic prayer in each rite. The Jewish theology that the church consecrates by giving thanks underlies the earliest stratum of each prayer. The reference in each prayer to the heavenly altar suggests that the bread and wine become the body and blood of Christ because the church's eucharist is a participation in the worship of heaven—the theology which underlies the incorporation of the Sanctus and the first epiclesis in the anaphora of St. Mark, whereas in the Roman canon the Sanctus represents an embellishment more than a structural element of theological significance. We turned our attention to this theology in chapter 3 above. In terms of the specific reference in both to God's acceptance of our offerings at the heavenly altar, the Letter to the Hebrews is especially important. The following texts in that epistle offer reference to those who made offerings which God accepted:

> ...being made perfect [Jesus] became the source of eternal salvation to all who obey him, being designated a high priest after the order of Melchizedek (5:9-10).

> By faith Abel offered to God a more acceptable sacrifice than Cain, through which he received approval as righteous, God bearing witness by accepting his gifts...(11:4).

> By faith Abraham, when he was tested, offered up Isaac, and he who had received the promises was ready to offer up his only son...(11:17).

The suggestion in the prayer that it is the ministry of angels to present the prayers and offerings of the church before God is rooted in the Old Testament, but we might think of the following verses from Revelation:

> And another angel came and stood at the altar with a golden censer; and he was given much incense to mingle with the prayers of the saints upon the golden altar before the throne; and the smoke of the incense rose with the prayers of the saints from the hand of the angel before God (8:3-4).

Thus it is that the two traditions suggest that our offerings are accepted at the throne of grace.

In the final form of St. Mark, it is the Spirit which is invoked upon the bread and wine which "makes" them the body and blood of Christ. The final theology of consecration is thus a West Syrian theology. The early form of the Roman canon which we find in Ambrose and Mozarabic sources still suggests that it is the church's sacramental participation in the worship of heaven that consecrates the bread and wine as the body and blood of Christ. Let us listen to the relevant texts: "graciously account their offering blessed, proper, and spiritual, for it is the image and likeness [or the figure] of the body and blood of Jesus Christ thy Son and our redeemer.... And we beg and pray thee that thou wouldst take this offering to thy altar on high, borne by the hands of thine angels...." Communion in Christ's body and blood is made possible because the bread and wine that are offered as the "image and likeness" or "figure" of Christ's body and blood have been received by God and united with the reality which they represent. In the final text of the Roman canon the first petition has been altered into a direct request that the church's offering "may become for us the body and blood of thy beloved son our Lord Jesus Christ...that as many as shall partake at this altar of the most holy body and blood of thy Son may be filled with every heavenly blessing and grace." In both the early and late forms of the canon the account of the institution and the words of Christ are a dependent clause subordinate to the petition for God to reckon the church's offering acceptable. It is this plea in the Roman tradition which takes the place of the epiclesis in Eastern traditions.

Yet even in the time of Ambrose the words of Christ in the institution account had become the focal point of the prayer for theologians. Ambrose suggests in his baptismal homily that it is the words of Christ which effect the consecration. This is a theology of consecration that is read into the text, for the text itself does not suggest it. Future developments in the theology of the eucharistic sacrifice and of eucharistic consecration were worked out not in the text of the eucharistic prayer but in rubrical regulations of liturgical gesture (most significantly in the late medieval rubric requiring the elevation of the elements for adoration after reciting the words of Christ), in the private devotions (*apologiae*) of the celebrant, in devotional commentaries and tracts, and in theological treatises and canonical decisions of ecclesiastical councils. These developments were imposed upon the text of the canon rather than being based on the text of the canon.

It is more difficult to speak of a theology of the eucharistic prayers of the Gallican and Mozarabic traditions because so much of their text is variable. What is clear is that the institution narrative takes on a consecratory function by default, because texts associating the consecration with participation in the worship of heaven or with the invocation of the Spirit may or may not be part of any particular set of eucharistic texts in these traditions.

NOTES

[1] Mazza, *The Origins of the Eucharist Prayer*, chapters 5 and 7.

[2] See the arguments presented by Mazza in *The Origins of the Eucharistic Prayer,* chapter 5, Geoffrey Cuming in "The Anaphora of St. Mark: A Study in Development," in *Museon* 95 (1982), pages 115-129, and *The Liturgy of St. Mark* (Rome: Pontificium Institutum Orientale, 1985), and by Herman Wegman in "Une anaphore incomplete? Les fragments sur Papyrus Strasbourg Gr. 254," in R. van den Broek and M. J. Vermaseren, eds., *Studies in Gnosticism and Hellenistic Religions* (Leiden: Brill, 1981), pages 432-450. Bryan Spinks argues against this conclusion in "A Complete Anaphora?", in *Heythorpe Journal* 25 (1984), 51-55.

[3] Enrico Mazza carefully sets out the materials in chapter 7 of *Origins of the Eucharistic Prayer*, which is the basis of the texts and translations in the remainder of this chapter.

[4] See the Greek text in Mazza, *Origins of the Eucharistic Prayer*, pages 275-279; English translation, Jasper and Cuming, *Prayers of the Eucharist*, pages 52-54; the text in the British Museum Tablet is found on pages 54-56; and of the final form of St. Mark on pages 57-66.

[5] Ibid, pages 54-56.

[6] Ibid., pages 57-66.

[7] Texts translated from the Latin in Mazza, *Origins of the Eucharistic Prayer*, chapter 7. For a convenient edition of the Latin text of the Roman canon, with an English translation and related documents, see Gordon P. Jeanes, *The Origins of the Roman Rite* (Bramcote, Notts.: Grove Books, 1991).

[8] Ibid.

[9] Ibid.

[10] Louis Ligier, unpublished manuscript, cited in Mazza, *The Origins of the Eucharistic Prayer*, page 254, note 50.

[11] On this, see Joseph A. Jungmann, *The Mass of the Roman Rite: Its Origins and Development* (Blackrock, Co. Dublin, Ireland: Four Courts Press, 1986), vol. 2, pages 101-109.

[12] For a brief description of the eucharistic prayers of these rites, along with English translations of sample prayers, see Jasper and Cuming, *Prayers of the Eucharist*, pages 147-154; Bouyer, *Eucharist*, pages 315-337; and Dix, *Shape of the Liturgy*, pages 551-563.

The Evolution of the Structure and Theology of the Eucharistic Prayer

❖ ❖ ❖ ❖ ❖ ❖ ❖ ❖ ❖ ❖ ❖ ❖ ❖

It is time for us to review what we have learned about the evolution of the eucharistic prayer and the theology implicit in its components. The evolution starts with a relatively simple and brief nucleus and then is expanded as new components are added to this nucleus — additions made at different times in different traditions and combined with the original nucleus in different ways.

1 and 2. The Nucleus: Thanksgiving and Supplication

At the last supper Jesus blessed the bread at the beginning of the meal and gave thanks over a cup of wine at the end of the meal. When the eucharist came to be celebrated as a sacramental meal in its own right (without other foods), the church eventually fused the blessings of bread and wine into a single eucharistic prayer, whose model seems to have been the blessing at the end of a Jewish meal, the *Birkat ha-Mazon*. While the Jewish name for such a prayer was blessing (*berakah* in Hebrew, eulogia in Greek), because the standard forms began by blessing God, Christians spoke of the prayer over the bread and wine as thanksgiving (*eucharistia* in Greek), because they began by *giving thanks* to God (like the second strophe of the *Birkat ha-Mazon*). The *Birkat ha-Mazon* consists of a strophe of blessing, a strophe of thanksgiving, and a final strophe of supplication. Its Christian analogue in chapter 10 of the *Didache* has two strophes of thanksgiving and a final strophe of supplication. The models provided by the *Birkat ha-Mazon* and the *Didache* can thus be outlined as follows:

Birkat ha-Mazon	*Didache*, **chapter 10**
Blessing	Thanksgiving
Thanksgiving	Thanksgiving
Supplication	Supplication

A similar pattern is seen in the early form of the anaphora of St. Mark found in the Strasbourg papyrus and in what appears to be the nucleus of other eucharistic prayers. The prayer opens with thanksgiving and concludes with supplication. The thanksgiving is brief and may at times be reduced to a single strophe; at other times the first of the two strophes takes the character of praise rather than thanksgiving. The original supplication appears to be a supplication for the church or the communicants, though in most cases it was expanded at an early date. It has been suggested by some that some early eucharistic prayers had no supplication. While this is possible, it rests on speculative reconstruction of the original nucleus of existing texts.

Such prayers understand the thanksgiving over the bread and wine at the sacramental meal to fulfill Jesus' command to do this in remembrance of him. The theology implicit in such prayers is that by giving thanks as we remember Jesus we restore the gifts of bread and wine to the purpose for which God intended them — as means of communion with God, now understood as communion with Christ. The prayer itself is understood as the church's sacrifice of praise and thanksgiving — a spiritual or rational sacrifice which takes the form of offering prayer rather than making material offerings. When the eucharistic prayer is understood in this way, the sacrificial interpretation of thanksgiving may be formulated as part of the thanksgiving. We find this in the second strophe of the preface in the Alexandrian anaphora of St. Mark and in the second strophe of many of the variable prefaces of the sacramentary of Verona in the Roman rite. Early apologists cite as the warrant not Deuteronomy 8:10 (the warrant for the Jewish table grace), but Malachi 1:11, which speaks of the pure offering which all the nations will make to God in the last days. The anaphora of St. Mark actually cites this text in its second strophe.

As the church defined itself over against the Gnostics who denied the goodness of creation, it came to associate the gifts of bread and wine with its sacrifice of praise and thanksgiving — an offering to God of the first-fruits of creation. This generally did not find expression in the original nucleus of the prayer, however, but in later additions. We find it in the anamnesis of the Byzantine anaphoras, where the church offers "*ta sa ek ton son*", and in the anamnesis of the Roman canon as an offering "*de tuis donis ac datis*" — a return to God of God's own gifts in thanksgiving.

Let us now look at the major components that were added to that original nucleus of thanksgiving and supplication and their theological function.

3. THE EXPANSION OF THE THANKSGIVING

The thanksgivings in the *Birkat ha-Mazon* and chapter 10 of the *Didache* are brief — two short strophes in each case. In the *Didache* we find the thanksgivings given a Christological reference, but neither the Jewish nor the Christian prayers incorporate a narrative thanksgiving — that is, a confession of the *mirabilia Dei*, the redemptive work of God. Since Christians understood the eucharist to be the church's anamnesis of Christ and the proclamation of his death (1 Corinthians 11:26) until he come again, many felt the need to expand the reference into a narrative of God's work of creation and salvation. Some early prayers do this succinctly, without expanding the length of the prayers. The thanksgiving remains quite brief in the fixed prefaces of the Syrian anaphora of the apostles (the text behind the later anaphoras of the Twelve Apostles and St. John Chrysostom), in the Alexandrian anaphora of St. Mark, and in the variable prefaces of the Roman rite. But the majority of the West Syrian anaphoras developed a substantial and often eloquent narrative, usually in the part of the eucharistic prayer that came after the Sanctus.

4. THE EXPANSION OF THE SUPPLICATION

The nucleus of the supplication is a prayer for the unity and peace of the church, which may also develop into a petition for the communicants. Later eucharistic prayers expanded this nucleus in two ways. The original supplication might first of all incorporate an invocation (epiclesis) of the Spirit as a part of the prayer for the church and the communicants. The final section of the anaphora of the *Apostolic Tradition* appears to have developed in this way. There was also a general tendency to duplicate in the supplication the scope of intercessions included earlier in the service in the prayers of the people. In some traditions (as in the anaphora of St. Basil) this simply took the form of petitions to remember groups of people and topics of concern. In others (as in the derivatives of the anaphora of the apostles and the Roman canon) the supplication developed into an offering of the eucharistic sacrifice for particular people and concerns. This gives to the Roman canon, where the thanksgiving was abbreviated and the supplication, formulated in terms of sacrifice, was vastly expanded, a thematic focus quite different from that of other eucharistic prayers.

5. A PARTICIPATION IN THE WORSHIP OF HEAVEN (THE SANCTUS)

The Sanctus appears to have entered the eucharistic prayer as a way of associating the church's eucharist with the worship of heaven of which it was the sacramental expression. In Jewish liturgy the Sanctus (*Qedushah*) had a similar function, and this text appears to have been incorporated into the eucharistic prayer to articulate this understanding of Christian worship. The Sanctus brought with it its introduction (joining the church's worship with the seraphic hymn) and sometimes an epiclesis (invoking God to join the church's worship with the worship of heaven). This association of the epiclesis with the Sanctus is most clearly seen in the Alexandrian anaphora of St. Mark, but the eucharistic prayer of Cyril of Jerusalem may have associated the epiclesis with the Sanctus in the same way. The Sanctus was incorporated into the eucharistic prayer in various ways. It might be prefaced (with preliminary praise of God and its introduction) to the original nucleus of a eucharistic prayer, it might be inserted in the middle of the original thanksgivings or at their end, or it might simply be appended to the prayer (as appears to have been the case at Alexandria). In some traditions it is integral to the eucharistic prayer, in others it has been incorporated into the prayer (or added on to it) but remains peripheral to its thematic structure.

In the Alexandrian and Roman traditions the church's participation in the worship of heaven is also signaled in the supplication by associating

the church's offering with the offerings of Abel, Abraham, and
Melchizedek, references drawn from the Letter to the Hebrews. The relevant text asks that the church's offering be brought to the heavenly
altar by the ministry of an angel (or angels).

6. THE EPICLESIS

The invocation of the Spirit appears to have developed as an
embolism on the Sanctus or as reworking of the supplication for the
church, but in later prayers it becomes an independent element. The
Spirit might be invoked upon the communicants, upon the elements, or
upon both. In earlier eucharistic prayers (such as that of Hippolytus and
the Alexandrian anaphora of St. Basil) the invocation upon the elements
is directed toward the sanctification of the communicants; in later
prayers it has a consecratory force, with a petition for the transformation of the elements into the body and blood of Christ. In many prayers
an oblation of the elements as the antitypes of Christ's body and blood
is incorporated into the epiclesis, thus associating the bread and wine
with Christ's sacrifice and expressing the relation between the church's
sacrifice and Christ's sacrifice in this way.

7. THE WARRANT: THE INSTITUTION NARRATIVE AND ANAMNESIS

The second paragraph of the *Birkat ha-Motzi* incorporates, in its
various versions, either an allusion to Deuteronomy 8:10 or a citation
of the text as the warrant for grace at the close of the meal. Some early
eucharistic prayers use Malachi 1:11 in the same way. 1 Corinthians
11:26 may have functioned in the same way in other prayers. But the
warrant incorporated into later eucharistic prayers is the account of the
last supper. This account concludes with Christ's command, "Do this in
remembrance of me," and so in eucharistic prayers it is usually coupled
with an expression of the church's intention that its eucharist should
fulfil that command: "remembering, we offer and/or we give thanks." It
is here that the association of the church's sacrifice of praise with the
bread and the cup is usually made.

In the classic West Syrian pattern the institution account and the
anamnesis come at the conclusion of the thanksgiving and are followed
by the epiclesis and the supplication. In the Alexandrian pattern, the
account, the anamnesis, and the epiclesis are simply appended to the
original nucleus of thanksgiving and supplication, which had already

been expanded with the Sanctus and an epiclesis. The Roman canon links the account and the anamnesis not with the thanksgiving narrative, but with the supplication, giving to this eucharistic prayer a distinctly different tone from what we find in the West Syrian tradition.

In the early Roman tradition, this supplication begins by asking God to accept the church's offering of bread and wine because they are the figure, the image, or the likeness of the body and blood of Christ, and then links the institution to this as a relative clause. The later form of this supplication asks God to accept the church's offering that it may become the body and blood of Christ, thus transforming a prayer for the acceptance of the offering into a prayer for the transformation of the offering and shifting the center of gravity of the whole prayer to the institution narrative.

The developed West Syrian structure seems most successful in crafting of all these elements a well ordered prayer and maintaining a theological balance between the many themes of its constituents. This is true although the relative uniformity of the final structure obscures the somewhat different courses of evolution which lie behind the various anaphoras. The structure might be set out as follows:

First Thanksgiving
Preface
    Praise of God in Alexandrian Basil
    Praise of the triune God in Byzantine Basil
    Praise of God as creator in James
    Thanksgiving for God's mighty deeds from the creation to the
        eschaton in Apostles
Pre-Sanctus
Sanctus

Second Thanksgiving
Post-Sanctus (linked to the Sanctus by the word "Holy")
    Praise for God's mighty deeds in Basil and James
    Transition to the Institution in the Apostles
Institution Narrative
Anamnesis with oblation and/or thanksgiving

Supplication
Invocation of the Spirit
Petition for the church
Other intercessions
Doxology

So attractive does this outline seem that many contemporary authors have sought to apply it to other traditions — equating the supplications for the acceptance of the offering before the institution narrative and after the anamnesis in the Roman tradition to the two epicleses of the Alexandrian structure, for example, and treating this as a minor variation of the West Syrian structure rather than as a very different structural outline. But the Roman canon and the Alexandrian anaphora of St. Mark (or St. Cyril) each have their own distinctive structure growing out of the way that the texts evolved and should not be interpreted as minor variants of a universal structure. In addition, the West Syrian structure really requires a comprehensive narrative of the economy of salvation in the preface or the post-Sanctus (though the narrative may take a brief summary form, as it does in the derivatives of the Syrian anaphora of the apostles) — something which is not found in the variable prefaces of the Western traditions. The Scottish American strand of the Anglican tradition after the Reformation is intentionally West Syrian in structure, but lacks such a narrative, making use of proper prefaces and including only the crucifixion in its post-Sanctus.

LOOKING TOWARD THE REFORMATION

By the late Middle Ages the institution narrative of the Roman canon had come to dominate the structure of the eucharistic prayer so greatly that it badly distorted the way in which the prayer and its theology were understood by most people. The element of thanksgiving had been reduced to a minimum, and its function was misinterpreted because the term "preface" was no longer understood as "solemn proclamation" of the church's praise and thanksgiving, but was now considered "preliminary matter" outside the canon. The original nucleus of the eucharistic prayer, the strophes of thanksgiving, were now treated as a kind of doxological prelude.

A theology of consecration had developed which understood the words of Christ as the "words of consecration" and tended to render the rest of the prayer superfluous for this purpose. Christ's presence in the elements was no longer understood as the instrumental means by which he united the communicants to himself as his body the Church, but as serving the purposes of adoration (for all worshipers) and of sanctification for those few who received communion. The eucharistic sacrifice was often understood not in terms of the church's sacrifice of thanksgiving or of its sacramental re-presentation of Christ's one sacrifice, but as a propitiatory sacrifice in its own right. The seeds of the disintegration of the eucharistic prayer in the churches of the Reformation had already been planted.

CHAPTER FIVE

THE REFORMATION AND THE LUTHERAN TRADITION

❖ ❖ ❖ ❖ ❖ ❖ ❖ ❖ ❖ ❖ ❖ ❖ ❖

To understand the eucharistic prayer (or rather, the lack of a eucharistic prayer) in the Lutheran reform of the eucharist, we need first to take into account the development of the Roman mass during the Middle Ages. The first development to take note of is the custom of the silent recitation of the eucharistic prayer from the end of the Sanctus until the final doxology. Silent recitation of prayers by the celebrant was already becoming customary in Eastern liturgical tradition by the sixth century—something which we know because the emperor Justinian legislated in vain against the custom in 565. But the custom did not prevail in the West until later: there is no mention of it in the *Ordo Romanus Primus* in the seventh century.

In the course of the middle ages it also became customary for the celebrant to recite private prayers of devotion (*apologiae*) at certain points in the eucharist. Of particular concern here are the sets of such apologiae recited during the offertory. Two different principles then are involved in silent recitation of prayers in the Roman mass: the silent recitation of the canon involved a prayer that was a constituent element of the eucharist; the silent recitation of the apologiae involved devotional adjuncts to the rite. Without a knowledge of the evolution of the rite, however, we are likely to understand both kinds of prayers recited silently as equivalent in origin—as accretions to the rite.

We need also to remember that a set of manual acts developed for the text of the institution narrative in the course of the middle ages that grew out of the belief that the celebrant consecrated the elements of bread and wine by acting in the person of Christ to recite the words of Christ. A final manual act which came into force late in the middle ages reinforced this understanding of consecration: immediately after speaking the words over the bread (and eventually after speaking the words over the chalice), the celebrant knelt in adoration, raised the bread (and eventually the cup) for the people to adore, and then knelt once again in adoration. To signal the beginning of the institution narrative (since the canon was recited silently after the Sanctus), it became customary to ring a bell to signal that the consecration was about to take place. When lengthy musical settings of the Sanctus became customary, the celebrant commenced the silent recitation of the canon during the first part of this hymn, recited the institution account in silence as the singers paused, and then continued to the end of the canon while they sang the rest of the hymn (the Benedictus qui venit). The institution narrative was thus set off from the rest of the canon. By the end of the middle ages, Latin Christians had in fact no very clear conception of just what constituted the eucharistic prayer. In the early middle ages the title, "Incipit canon actionis," had been moved from the true beginning of the prayer—before the preface—to a position after the Sanctus, thus suggesting that the preceding text was not part of the canon. The termination of various sections of the canon, "through Christ our Lord. Amen," also suggested a series of prayers rather than a single eucharistic prayer.

Whereas in the early centuries all members of the congregation would have received communion unless they were under ecclesiastical discipline, by the late middle ages no one would have communicated except the celebrant (and perhaps a few of his assistants). This quite naturally suggested that Christ was present in the elements primarily for adoration rather than for communion. The act of communion was generally understood as effecting union with Christ rather than union with Christ and one's fellow Christians within the body of the church.

The dominance of sacrificial language in the Roman canon coupled with the doctrine of consecration by the words of Christ also led to a new understanding of the sacrificial language of the eucharist. Several of the references to sacrifice in the Roman canon come after the institution narrative. The location of these references in the canon (rather than the actual wording of the references) suggested that what was offered in sacrifice was Christ himself and that each celebration of the eucharist was a new sacrifice of Christ on behalf of those for whom the eucharist was offered.

Luther's instinct in reforming the eucharist seems to have been to remove secondary accretions to the rite. The principle by which he determined what was secondary was public recitation: those texts recited silently were secondary accretions. His 1523 Latin rite, the *Formula Missae et Communionis*, thus simply removed all texts recited silently. Of course the institution narrative was also recited silently, but Luther understood the words of Christ in this narrative to effect the consecration of the elements, so he retained them and directed that they be sung to a prayer tone. A congregation attending a celebration of this rite would see and hear the same rite for the eucharist to which it had long been accustomed, with the additional public recitation of the institution narrative (now placed at the end of the first strophe of the preface, before the Sanctus). The 1526 German rite was somewhat more radical, eliminating the preface and replacing it with a paraphrase of the Lord's Prayer and an exhortation. The key change, however, is more subtle: the institution narrative was to be sung to a gospel tone.[1] The elements were now understood to be consecrated not by a eucharistic prayer but by the proclamation of the gospel. In the German Mass Luther did not revise the eucharistic prayer, he eliminated it altogether! This action, radical as it may seem, is really only the logical consequence of the theology of consecration by the words of Christ already set out in the late fourth century by Ambrose in his baptismal homilies.

Luther tells us very clearly why he has done this in the text which accompanies the directions given in the *Formula Missae*: the text of eucharistic liturgy from the offertory on [i.e., the apologiae at the offertory and the canon] "smacks and savors of sacrifice." Luther's reforms were precipitated by his reaction to the medieval doctrine that the mass as a sacrifice was a "good work" which could be offered on behalf of the living and the dead. From his perspective it was the words of Christ that were the primary text here: the rest of the canon was a secondary accretion which gave expression to a false theology of the eucharistic sacrifice. While the language of sacrifice does indeed dominate (and, we might argue, unbalance) the Roman canon, the late medieval doctrine of eucharistic sacrifice was read into the text rather than read out of it. The use of the language of Hebrews in the supplication for the acceptance of the sacrifice after the institution narrative suggests that the church's praise and thanksgiving and its offering of bread and wine "from the gifts God has bestowed upon us" are the sacramental means by which Christ's own sacrifice is made present to the church and united with the church's offering. This indeed is consistent with the doctrine of sacrifice which Luther set out in his early eucharistic tract, the *Treatise on the New Testament.* But this congruence was not apparent to anyone who read the text of the canon from a late medieval perspective.

Both the traditional appearance of the Lutheran rite and its internally radical character can be seen by setting out the structure of the Roman rite, the Latin rite of 1523, and the German rite of 1526 in parallel columns, marking text for which music is provided with an asterisk. When we do this it becomes rapidly apparent that the congregation saw and heard (in Latin or in German) in the rites of 1523 and 1526 almost exactly what they had seen and heard in the Roman rite, but that the eucharistic prayer, the central text of the celebration, had disappeared. But since it had been recited silently in the Roman rite, its disappearance did not alter the external appearance of the eucharist for the congregation. A genuinely radical alteration of the eucharist had been carried out with almost no external change.

A COMPARISON OF THE ROMAN MASS AND LUTHER'S LATIN AND GERMAN MASSES

I. THE LITURGY OF THE WORD

Roman Mass	Luther's Latin Mass	German Mass
Silent devotions of the Ministers before the Altar		
*Introit psalm verses	*Introit verses or psalm	*Full introit psalm or hymn
*9-fold "Lord, have mercy"	*"Lord, have mercy"	*3-fold "Lord, have mercy"
*"Glory to God" if appointed	*"Glory to God" if appointed	
*Greeting and collect	*Greeting and collect	*Greeting and collect
*Epistle	*Epistle	*Epistle (rule for chant)
*Gradual and alleluia verses	*Gradual /alleluia verses	
*Sequence or prose	[*Sequences discouraged*]	*German Hymn
*Gospel	*Gospel	*Gospel (rules for chant)
*Nicene Creed	*Nicene Creed	*Metrical Creed
Sermon	Sermon [*or before service*]	Sermon

II. THE LITURGY OF THE TABLE

Roman Mass	Luther's Latin Mass	German Mass
*Offertory Sentence		
Preparation of bread and wine	*Preparation of bread and wine*	
Silent offertory prayers		
Silent offertory collect with ending sung aloud		
*"Lift up your hearts"	*"Lift up your hearts"	Paraphrase of Lord's Prayer
*Preface: "It is very meet"	*Preface: "It is very meet"	Communion Exhortation
*Continuation of Preface	*Narrative of last supper (set to tone of Lord's Prayer)	*Narrative of last supper (set to reading tone)
*"Holy. holy, holy"	*Holy, holy, holy"	[*Note: Luther suggests that the bread word of the narrative may be sung before distribution of the bread and the cup word before distribution of the cup*]
*"Blessed is he who comes"	*"Blessed is he who comes"	
Silent recitation of remainder of the canon		
*Sung conclusion of doxology		
*Lord's Prayer with introduction	*Lord's Prayer with introduction	
Fraction		
*"The peace of the Lord be always with you."	*"The Peace of the Lord be always with you"	*Metrical "Holy, holy, holy" and "Lamb of God" during communion and/or Huss's "Jesus Christ our Savior" and/or "Praise to God"
*"Lamb of God" *and silent communion devotions*	*"Lamb of God" during communion	
*Communion verse	*Optional communion verse	
*Variable postcommunion	*Fixed postcommunion	Fixed postcommunion
*Dismissal	*"Let us bless the Lord"	
*Blessing	*Old or Aaronic blessing	Aaronic blessing

Let us look at the texts which replaced the Roman canon in these two rites of Luther's:[2]

LUTHER'S LATIN MASS

Dialogue and First Part of Preface

V. The Lord be with you.

R. And with thy spirit.

V. Lift up your hearts.

R. We lift them up unto the Lord.

V. Let us give thanks unto our Lord God.

R. It is meet and right.

It is truly meet and right, fitting and salutary, that we should at all times and in all places give thanks unto thee, O Lord, holy Father, almighty, everlasting God through Christ our Lord:

Institution Narrative

Who on the day before he suffered took bread and, when he had given thanks, broke it, and gave it to his disciples, saying, "Take this, eat: This is my body, which is given for you." In the same manner also the cup, when he had supped, saying, "This cup is the new testament in my blood which is shed for you and for many for the forgiveness of sins. Whenever you do this, do it in remembrance of me."

GERMAN MASS

Exhortation

...I admonish you in Christ that you discern the Testament of Christ in true faith and, above all, take to heart the words wherein Christ imparts to us his body and his blood for the remission of our sins; that you remember and give thanks for his boundless love which he proved to us when he redeemed us from God's wrath, sin, death, and hell by his own blood; and that in this faith you externally receive the bread and wine, that is, his body and blood, as the pledge and guarantee of this. In his name, therefore, and according to the command that he gave, let us use and receive the testament.

The Office and Consecration

Our Lord Jesus Christ, in the night in which he was betrayed, took bread; and when he had given thanks, he broke it and gave it to his disciples, saying, "Take, eat: this is my body, which is given for you; do this in remembrance of me." After the same manner also, he took the cup, when he had supped, and when he had given thanks, he gave it to them, saying, "Drink this, all of you: this cup is the new testament in my blood, which is shed for you and for many for the forgiveness of sins. Do this, as often as you drink it, in remembrance of me."

With the reduction of the eucharistic prayer to the preface and institution narrative in the Latin mass and its abolition in the German mass, there was little way to articulate a theology of the eucharist within the text of the rite. We can discern Luther's eucharistic theology from other writings,[3] but there was no adequate way to bring this theology to expression in the celebration of the eucharist. Let us examine this theology, comparing it to the theology of earlier prayers and seeing how it may have shaped the rite and found expression in it. We begin with the theme of thanksgiving, which gave the name eucharistia to the rite.

Luther's Latin rite (and its descendents in Lutheran church orders) retained the beginning of the preface, which is an expression of thanksgiving. However, the classical prefaces gave thanks for the saving deeds of Christ. Unless a proper preface is used, however, Luther's rite, where the first part of the preface leads into the institution narrative, suggests that the thanksgiving is for the institution of the eucharist, and in the *Treatise on the New Testament* Luther writes that "we are to offer him our praise and thanksgiving with our whole heart, for his unspeakable, sweet grace and mercy, which he has promised and given us in this sacrament." But he immediately goes on to add that "such a sacrifice does not necessarily and essentially belong to the mass...."[4] And so the preface disappeared from the German mass. The exhortation which introduces the gospel of the last supper ("the testament") in the German mass replaces the corporate thanksgiving of the preface with an exhortation to individual thanksgiving. This replacement of the eucharistic prayer with exhortation and the account of the institution would be characteristic of many rites in this period (though in the Reformed tradition the institution would be understood as warrant rather than as consecration).

Christ's presence is a preeminent theme of Lutheran theology. Luther's greatest concern was to secure a real and substantial presence of Christ's body and blood in, with, and under the species of bread and wine. His disputation with Zwingli hinged on this concern. In classical eucharistic prayers this theme finds expression in the supplication of the Roman rite which introduces the institution narrative and asks that the bread and wine *may become* Christ's body and blood and in the epiclesis of Eastern rites, which asks God to send the Holy Spirit to make the elements Christ's body and blood. No such prayer is a part of either of Luther's rites, but the institution narrative itself is used in such a way as to give indirect expression to the theme.

Christ is present for the purposes of communion in both the older rites and in Luther's rite. The classic rites understand communion in a twofold way: it unites individual Christians to Christ so that they may enjoy the benefits of communion, which are spelled out in the prayers; and it unites individual Christians to their fellow Christians so that they become one body in Christ. This twofold understanding of communion is evident in Luther's early work, *The Blessed Sacrament of the Holy and True Body of Christ, and the Brotherhoods*, where he says:

> Just as the bread is made out of many grains ground and mixed together, and out of the bodies of many grains there comes the body of one bread, in which each grain loses its form and body and takes upon itself the common body of the bread; and just as the drops of wine, in losing their own form, become the body of one common wine and drink—so it is and should be with us, if we use this sacrament properly. Christ with all his saints, by his love, takes upon himself our form, fights with us against sin, death, and all evil. This enkindles in us such love that we take on his form, rely upon his righteousness, life, and blessedness. And through the interchange of his blessings and our misfortunes, we become one loaf, one bread, one body, one drink, and have all things in common. O this is a great sacrament, says St. Paul, that Christ and the church are one flesh and bone.[5]

Luther concludes his exposition of the meaning of the eucharist by explicitly setting out this corporate dimension of the rite:

> This fellowship is twofold: on the one hand we partake of Christ and all saints; on the other hand we permit all Christians to be partakers of us, in whatever way they and we are able. Thus by means of this sacrament, all self-seeking love is rooted out and gives place to that which seeks the common good of all; and through the change wrought by love there is one bread, one drink, one body, one community.[6]

The corporate understanding of communion disappears from Luther's later works, and his focus is almost exclusively on the benefit to the individual communicant. The individual sense alone finds expression in the Exhortation of the German rite and in Luther's treatment of the sacrament of the altar in his shorter catechism.

One of Luther's primary goals in his revisions was to remove any suggestion that the eucharist is a sacrifice. His instinct was to replace the theme of sacrifice with that of testament (as legacy), as is indicated by his first major work on the topic, *A Treatise on the New Testament,* and in the exhortation of his German rite. This finds expression in Luther's substitute for the eucharistic prayer, the biblical account of the last supper, which speaks of Christ's blood of the new testament (though the sense of the word in this context is really that of covenant rather than testament). In the exhortation and in the shorter catechism Christians are instructed that Christ's legacy to them is the forgiveness of sins, received in the reception of Christ's body and blood given for *thee* (Luther uses the singular here, where the biblical accounts use the plural—a fact disguised in the standard English translations) for the forgiveness of sins. The testator has given us his body and blood as a sign of this legacy.

In his *Treatise on the New Testament, that is, the Holy Mass,* however, Luther was willing to speak of the sense in which the eucharist may be understood as a sacrifice, working from an exegesis of the letter to the Hebrews:

> What sacrifices, then, are we to offer? Ourselves, and all that we have, with constant prayer, as we say, "Thy will be done, on earth as it is in heaven." With this we are to yield ourselves up to the will of God, that he may make of us what he will, according to his pleasure. In addition we are to offer him praise and thanksgiving with our whole heart, for his unspeakable, sweet grace and mercy, which he has promised and given us in this sacrament. And although such a sacrifice occurs apart from the mass, and should so occur—for it does not necessarily and essentially belong to the mass, as has been said—yet it is more precious, more appropriate, more mighty, and also more acceptable when its takes place with the multitude and in the assembly, where men encourage, move, and inflame one another to press close to God and thereby attain without any doubt what they desire....
>
> To be sure this sacrifice of prayer, praise, and thanksgiving, and of ourselves as well, we are not to present before God in our own person. But we are to lay it upon Christ and let him present it for us, as St. Paul teaches in Hebrews 13:15, "Let us continually offer up a sacrifice of praise to God, that is, the fruit of lips that confess him and praise him;" and all this "through Christ." For this is why he is also a priest, as Psalm 110:4 says, "You are a priest for ever after the order of Melchizedek"—because he intercedes for us in heaven. He receives our prayer and sacrifice, and through himself, as a godly priest, makes them pleasing to God. Again St. Paul says in Hebrews 9:24, "He has ascended into heaven to be a mediator in the presence of God on our behalf;" and in Romans 8:34, "It is Christ Jesus, who died, yes, who was raised from the dead, who sits on the right hand of God, who also makes intercession for us."
>
> From these words we learn that we do not offer Christ as a sacrifice, but that Christ offers us. And in this way it is permissible, yea, profitable, to call the mass a sacrifice, not on its own account, but because we offer up ourselves as a sacrifice along with Christ. That is to say, we lay ourselves on Christ by a firm faith in his testament and do not otherwise appear before God with our prayer, praise, and sacrifice except through Christ and his mediation.[7]

This sacramental union with Christ in his self-offering in the heavenly sanctuary finds expression in the allusion to Hebrews in the Roman canon, but with the excision of the canon there is no place for it to find expression in Luther's rites.

It would certainly be possible to construct a eucharistic prayer along traditional lines which articulated the positive expression of

Luther's doctrine of eucharistic sacrifice and eucharistic presence, but Luther had only the model of the Roman canon before him, and in that text the language of sacrifice and oblation is so dominant that Luther made no attempt to revise it. We do find such an attempt in the German paraphrase of the Roman canon of the Wormser deutsche Messe of 1524/1525[8] and in the skillful English adaptation of Thomas Cranmer, Anglican Archbishop of Canterbury, in 1549. In Sweden, the Lutheran reformers produced somewhat more adequate eucharistic prayers at certain stages of that church's history. But in the Lutheran tradition as a whole, the eucharistic prayer disappeared, replaced by the recitation of the narrative of the last supper read as a gospel; and by its nature this text could not articulate the traditional themes of the eucharistic prayer. Jesus took bread and wine at the last supper, gave thanks, and distributed them to his disciples as his body and blood. Luther sought to construct a eucharistic rite that was faithful to the gospel, but failed to notice that by eliminating the thanksgiving he created a rite that did not conform to the norm of the gospel.

NOTES

[1] Luther also recommended the separate consecration and distribution of the bread and wine, but this procedure proved cumbersome and was generally abandoned in later church orders.

[2] Texts taken from the English translations in Ulrich Leupold, ed., *Luther's Works*, vol. 53, *Liturgy and Hymns*, (Philadelphia: Fortress Press, 1965), pages 19-40 (Latin Mass) and 68-90 (German Mass); translations slightly adapted. The German mass gives tones for the psalm, the epistle, the gospel, and the institution narrative.

[3] The classic interpretation of Luther's eucharistic theology is found in Yngve Brilioth, *Eucharistic Faith and Practice: Evangelical and Catholic*, trans. A. G. Hebert (London: SPCK, 1961). Chapter IV and VII of this book are devoted to the Lutheran tradition. For a brief contemporary treatment, see William R. Crockett, *Eucharist: Symbol of Transformation* (New York: Pueblo, 1989), chapter 4.

[4] For the full text, see below.

[5] Translation in E. Theodore Bachman, ed., *Luther's Works*, vol. 35, *Word and Sacrament I* (Philadelphia: Muhlenberg Press, 1960), pages 49-73, here page 58.

[6] Ibid., page 67.

[7] Translation ibid., pages 79-111, here pages 98-99.

[8] For the German text of this eucharistic prayer and an English translation, see Herman Wegman, *Christian Worship in East and West: A Study Guide to Liturgical History* (New York: Pueblo, 1985), pages 322-325.

CHAPTER SIX

THE REFORMED TRADITION
THE LORD'S SUPPER

❖ ❖ ❖ ❖ ❖ ❖ ❖ ❖ ❖ ❖ ❖ ❖ ❖

ULRICH ZWINGLI AT ZURICH

The early reformed rites for the eucharist are contemporaneous with Luther's rites. Ulrich Zwingli produced a rather conservative revision in 1523, as Luther did that same year. Unlike Luther, Zwingli provided in this rite a series of prayers to replace the canon of the mass. These prayers bear little resemblance to the Roman canon, but they do include a recital of God's acts of creation and redemption such as we find in West Syrian anaphoras. The eucharistic doctrine implicit in these prayers is ambiguous. They declare that Christ gave himself to us as our food and drink, but they also declare that the only spiritual food that can refresh our souls is God's Word. In 1525 Zwingli produced a far more radical rite which gave expression to a quite different eucharistic theology from that of Martin Luther. The Lutheran reformation had no intention of abolishing the weekly Sunday eucharist, as the apology for the Augsburg confession declares; but Zwingli stipulated only a quarterly celebration—at Christmas, Easter, Pentecost, and once in the fall. Luther retained the traditional ceremonial, music, and vestments, though he considered them adiaphora; Zwingli abolished them all.

Luther's rites of 1523 and 1526 both followed the traditional structure of the eucharist in the West. Zwingli's final rite tacked the Lord's supper onto his regular Sunday service, which took the shape of the traditional vernacular devotions (the prone) which had long been inserted in the middle of the Latin rite. The prone, or vernacular pulpit service, popular in Switzerland, Southern Germany, and elsewhere, often included a lesson from Scripture in the vernacular, a sermon, biddings and prayers in the vernacular, and sometimes vernacular hymns.

The form for the Lord's Supper in Zwingli's 1525 rite makes manifest the radical nature of his reform. A brief ministry of the word with eucharistic lessons is attached to the preaching service. This is followed by an exhortation to a devout communion which leads into the Lord's Prayer. A prayer of humble access follows. Then the account of the institution is read as a warrant and the elements are distributed. There is no consecration because Zwingli dissociates the elements from Christ's body and blood, which cannot be present because Christ has ascended into heaven. Zwingli's eucharist is a meal at the Lord's table. But the meal lacks a grace!

Zwingli has received harsh treatment at the hands of later interpreters for his eucharistic theology. But there was also a positive thrust to his theology.[1] He speaks of the corporate dimension of the eucharist in the way that Luther did in his early treatise, *The Blessed Sacrament of the Holy and True Body of Christ*, but while Luther ignored this theme in his later work, it became a major theme of Zwingli's eucharistic theology: the true goal of the eucharist is to transform the church into the body of Christ. Thus he writes:

> As bread is made up of many grains and wine of many grapes, so by a common trust in Christ which proceeds from the one Spirit the body of the Church is constituted and built up out of many members a single body, to be the true temple of the indwelling Spirit.[2]

And while he did not believe that the communicant received the body and blood of Christ through the sacramental signs of bread and wine, he could speak very eloquently, nonetheless, of their significance:

> With the sight we see the bread and wine which in Christ's stead signify his goodness and favorable disposition. Is it not therefore the handmaid of faith? For it sees Christ before it as it were, and the soul is enflamed by his beauty and loves him more dearly. With the sense of touch we take the bread into our hand and in signification it is no longer bread but Christ. And there is also a place for taste and smell in order that we may taste and see how good the Lord is and how blessed is the man that trusts in him: for just as the senses take pleasure in good and are stimulated by it, so the soul exults and rejoices when it tastes the sweet savor of the heavenly hope.[3]

Zwingli's rhetorical elegance was not matched by his liturgical skill, however. In a way that was to be characteristic for the Reformed tradition, his rite replaced the eucharistic prayer of thanksgiving with an exhortation, and the account of the institution was read as a warrant for the celebration, not as a form of consecration (as it had been in Luther's German mass). The rite itself did not give any adequate expression to the eucharist as a means of building up the body of the church—a goal of which Zwingli spoke so eloquently elsewhere.

JOHN CALVIN AT GENEVA

Zwingli's eucharistic theology did not ultimately prevail in the Reformed tradition, however. Other reformers were not content with his minimalist theology, and it was John Calvin who was the preeminent theologian of the eucharist in this tradition.[4] Like Zwingli's, Calvin's eucharistic theology had a strong ecclesial dimension. He lists union with Christ as the first fruit of the Lord's Supper, and understands that union in a corporate sense:

> For the Lord so communicates his body to us there that he is made completely one with us and we with him. Now, since he has only one body, of which he makes us all partakers, it is necessary that all of us also be made one body by such participation. The bread shown in the Sacrament represents this unity. As it is made of many grains so mixed together that one cannot be distinguished from another, so it is fitting that in the same way we should be joined and bound together by such great agreement of mind that no sort of dis- agreement or division may intrude…. Accordingly, Augustine with good reason frequently calls this sacrament "the bond of love." For what sharper goad could there be to arouse mutual love among us than when Christ, giving himself to us, not only invites us by his own example to pledge and give ourselves to one another, but inas- much as he makes himself common to all, also makes all of us one in himself.

Calvin was as concerned as Zwingli was to deny a local or bodily presence of Christ in the elements of bread and wine, arguing that Christ's corporal presence was in heaven after his ascension and that to localize that presence in the bread and wine would put Christ at our dis- posal in a way that violated the sovereignty of God. But Calvin was equally concerned to argue that the bread and wine of the eucharist were not bare signs, but signs which offered to faithful communicants the reality which they represented, so that they really partook of the body and blood of Christ. For Calvin, it was the Holy Spirit which made this possible, for "the Spirit truly unites things separated in space" and therefore Christ "truly offers and shows the reality there signified to all who sit at that spiritual banquet, although it is received with benefit by believers alone.... If it is true that a visible sign is given us to seal the gift of a thing invisible, when we have received the symbol of the body, let us no less surely trust that the body itself is also given to us."[5] The signs are the instrumental cause of the presence, but they do not contain what they make present. Calvin insists that both the distinction and the union of the sacramental sign and the reality which it represents be acknowledged: "We have then to confess that if the representation which God grants in the supper is veracious, the internal substance of the sacrament is joined with the visible signs; and as the bread is distributed by hand, so the body of Christ is communicated to us, so that we are made partakers of it."[6] The Spirit makes this participation possible, not by bringing the ascended Christ down into our midst, but by raising us up to the presence of Christ in heaven.

Calvin repudiated what he understood to be the medieval doctrine of the eucharistic sacrifice, and in general he avoided sacrificial language for the eucharist. But he was also willing to concede that there were senses in which that language could be legitimate. He speaks of two kinds of sacrifices: the sacrifice of expiation and the sacrifice of praise, reverence, and thanksgiving. He cites Augustine as a representative patristic authority, first of all, to argue that the eucharist is a "a memorial, an image, and a testimony of that singular, true, and unique sacrifice by which Christ has atoned for us."[7] He can say, "we do not deny that the sacrifice of Christ is [in the Lord's Supper] so shown to us that the spectacle of the cross is almost set before our eyes...."[8]

The sacrifice of praise and thanksgiving "has nothing to do with appeasing God's wrath, with obtaining forgiveness of sins, but is concerned solely with magnifying and exalting God."[9] This kind of sacrifice, he declares, involves our self-oblation, "for Paul bids us 'offer our bodies a living sacrifice, holy, acceptable to God, a reasonable worship.'"[10] In conclusion, he relates this kind of sacrifice to the eucharist:

> The Lord's Supper cannot be without a sacrifice of this kind, in which, while we proclaim his death and give thanks, we do nothing but offer a sacrifice of praise. From this office of sacrificing, all Christians are called a royal priesthood, because through Christ we offer that sacrifice of praise to God of which the apostle speaks: "the fruit of lips confessing his name." And we do not appear before God without an intercessor. The Mediator interceding for us is Christ, by whom we offer ourselves and what is ours to the Father. He is our Pontiff, who has entered the heavenly sanctuary and

opens a way for us to enter. He is the altar upon which we lay our gifts, that whatever we venture to do, we may undertake in him. He it is, I say, that has made us a kingdom of priests unto the Father.[11]

Unlike Zwingli, Calvin considered the Lord's Supper part of the proper worship of every Lord's Day. He declared that "the Lord's Table should have been spread at least once a week for the assembly of Christians...."[12] Calvin inherited his rite for the Lord's Supper from Martin Bucer when he was minister of the French congregation during his exile in Strasbourg. The rite was as spare and severe as Zwingli's, and gave little scope for expression of the eucharistic theology of which we have taken note. In the *Institutes* Calvin sets out his ideal for the celebration:

> First, then it should begin with public prayers. After this a sermon should be given. Then, when bread and wine have been placed on the Table, the minister should repeat the words of institution of the supper. Next, he should recite the promises which were left to us in it; at the same time, he should excommunicate all who are debarred from it by the Lord's prohibition. Afterward, he should pray that the Lord, with the kindness wherewith he has bestowed this sacred food upon us, also teach and form us to receive it with faith and thankfulness of heart, and, inasmuch as we are not so of ourselves, by his mercy make us worthy of such a feast. But here either psalms should be sung, or something be read, and in becoming order the believers should partake of the most holy banquet, the ministers breaking the bread and giving the cup. When the Supper is finished, there should be an exhortation to sincere faith and confession of faith, to love and behavior worthy of Christians. At the last, thanks should be given, and praises sung to God. When these things are ended, the church should be dismissed in peace.[13]

Calvin's Genevan rite was appended to the conclusion of the intercessions of the Sunday preaching service. This is the text of that rite:

> *On those days when the Lord's Supper is to be celebrated, that which follows is joined to the preceding [prayer of intercession]:*
>
> And as our Lord Jesus has not only offered his body and blood once on the Cross for the remission of our sins, but also desires to impart them to us as our nourishment unto everlasting life, grant us this grace: that we may receive at his hands such a great benefit and gift with true sincerity and ardent zeal. In steadfast faith may we receive his body and blood, yea Christ himself entire, who being true God and true man, is verily the holy bread of heaven which gives us life. So may we live no longer in ourselves, after our nature which is entirely corrupt and vicious, but may he live in us and lead us to the life that is holy, blessed, and everlasting: whereby we may truly become partakers of the new and eternal testament, the covenant of grace, assured that it is thy good pleasure to be our gracious Father

forever, never reckoning our faults against us, and to provide for us, as thy well-beloved children and heirs, all our needs both of body and soul. Thus may we render praise and thanks unto thee without ceasing and magnify thy name in word and deed.

Grant us, therefore, O heavenly Father, so to celebrate this day the blessed memorial and remembrance of thy dear son, to exercise ourselves in the same, and to proclaim his death, that, receiving new growth and strength in faith and in all things good, we may with so much greater confidence proclaim thee our Father and glory in thee. Amen.

Then, having made the prayers and the Confession of Faith (which is to testify in the name of the people that they all wish to live and die in the Christian doctrine and religion), he says in a loud voice:

Let us hear how Jesus Christ instituted his holy Supper for us, as St. Paul relates it in the eleventh chapter of First Corinthians:

I have received of the Lord, he says, that which I have delivered unto you: that the Lord Jesus, on the night in which he was betrayed, took bread: And when he had given thanks, he broke it and said, "Take, eat; this is my body which is broken for you: this do in remembrance of me." After the same manner, when he had supped, he took the cup, saying, "This cup is the new testament in my blood: do this, as often as you shall drink it, in remembrance of me." For as often as you eat this bread and drink this cup, you proclaim the Lord's death until he come. Therefore, whosoever shall eat this bread and drink this cup unworthily shall be guilty of the body and blood of the Lord. But let a man examine himself and so let him eat of this bread and drink of this cup. For whosoever eats and drinks unworthily takes his own condemnation, not discerning the Lord's body.

We have heard, my brethren, how our Lord observed his Supper with his disciples, from which we learn that strangers and those who do not belong to the company of his faithful people must not be admitted. Therefore, following that precept, in the name and by the authority of our Lord Jesus Christ, I excommunicate all idolaters, blasphemers, and despisers of God, all heretics and those who create private sects in order to break the unity of the Church, all perjurers, all who rebel against father or mother or superior, all who promote sedition or mutiny, brutal and disorderly persons, adulterers, lewd and lustful men, thieves, ravishers, greedy and grasping people, drunkards, gluttons, and all those who lead a scandalous and dissolute life. I warn them to abstain from this Holy Table, lest they defile and contaminate the holy food which our Lord Jesus Christ gives to none except they belong to his household of faith.

Moreover, in accordance with the exhortation of St. Paul, let every man examine and prove his own conscience to see whether he truly repents of his faults and grieves over his sins, desiring to live henceforth a holy life according to God. Above all, let him see whether he has his trust in the mercy of God and seeks his salvation wholly in Jesus Christ and, renouncing all hatred and rancor, has high resolve and courage to live in peace and brotherly love with his neighbors.

If we have this witness in our hearts before God, never doubt that he claims us as his children, and that the Lord Jesus addresses his Word to us, to invite us to his Table and to give us this holy Sacrament which he imparted to his disciples.

And yet, we may be conscious of much frailty and misery in ourselves, such that we do not have perfect faith, but are inclined toward defiance and unbelief, or that we do not devote ourselves wholly to the service of God and with such zeal as we ought, but have to fight daily against the lusts of our flesh. Nevertheless, since our Lord has granted us the grace of having his gospel graven on our hearts, so that we may withstand all unbelief and has given us the desire and longing to renounce our own wishes, that we may follow his righteousness and his holy commandments: let us be assured that the sins and imperfections which remain in us will not prevent him from receiving us and making us worthy partakers of this spiritual Table. For we do not come here to testify that we are perfect or righteous in ourselves: On the contrary, by seeking our life in Jesus Christ we confess that we are in death. Know, therefore, that his Sacrament is a medicine for the poor sick souls, and that the only worthiness which our Lord requires of us is to know ourselves sufficiently to deplore our sins, and to find all our pleasure, joy, and satisfaction in him alone.

Above all, therefore let us believe those promises which Jesus Christ, who is the unfailing truth, has spoken with his own lips. He is truly willing to make us partakers of his body and blood, in order that we may possess him wholly and in such wise that he may live in us and we in him. And though we see but bread and wine, we must not doubt that he accomplishes spiritually in our souls all that he shows us outwardly by these visible signs, namely, that he is the bread of heaven to feed and nourish us unto eternal life. So, let us never be unmindful of the infinite goodness of our Savior who spreads out all his riches and blessing on this Table, to impart them to us. For in giving himself to us, he makes a testimony to us that all that he has is ours. Therefore, let us receive this Sacrament as a pledge that the virtue of his death and passion is imparted to us for righteousness, even as though we had suffered them in our own persons. May we never be so perverse as to draw away when Jesus Christ invites us so gently by his Word. But accounting the worthiness of this precious gift which he gives, let us present ourselves to him with ardent zeal, that he may make us capable of receiving it.

To do so, let us lift our spirits and hearts on high where Jesus Christ is in the glory of his Father, whence we expect him at our redemption. Let us not be fascinated by these earthly and corruptible elements which we see with our eyes and touch with our hands, seeking him there as though he were enclosed in the bread or wine.

Then only shall our souls be disposed to be nourished and vivified by his substance when they are lifted up above all earthly things, attaining even to heaven, and entering the kingdom of God where he dwells. Therefore let us be content to have the bread and wine as signs and witnesses, seeking the truth spiritually where the Word of God promises that we shall find it.

That done, the Ministers distribute the bread and the chalice to the people... [14]

The Lord's Supper here is framed in prayer—the special conclusion of the intercessions and the postcommunion prayer of thanksgiving (not given above). It includes the warrant, which opens the exhortation. But prayer and thanksgiving pale to insignificance in comparison with the penitential and controversial material of the exhortation, which dominates in Calvin's rite. The opening prayer sets out the theme of the eucharistic presence, but although Calvin elsewhere attributes Christ's presence to the work of the Holy Spirit that work finds no recognition at all in the prayer. The scope of thanksgiving is relatively restricted and occurs mostly in the postcommunion prayer. Calvin's repudiation of the medieval doctrine of eucharistic sacrifice was so strong that the church's thankful sacrifice of self-oblation found no place in the rite, though he considered it integral to the meaning of the Lord's Supper. It would fall to his later heirs to create a eucharistic liturgy which gave more adequate expression to his eucharistic theology.

JOHN KNOX IN SCOTLAND

John Knox, whose *Form of Prayers* became the eucharistic rite for the reformed Church of Scotland in *The Book of Common Order*, retained the basic structure of Calvin's liturgy, but provided what that rite lacked—a form of eucharistic prayer. Elements of his rite come from Cranmer's Book of Common Prayer, though he rejected the liturgical form of that rite. He began, as Calvin did, with a reading of the text of the warrant for the celebration from 1 Corinthians and an exhortation. But when the exhortation was ended, he moved from the pulpit to the table and continued with the following prayer.

O Father of mercy and God of all consolation, seeing all creatures do [ac]knowledge and confess thee, as governor and Lord, it becometh us the workmanship of thine own hands, at all times to reverence and magnify thy godly majesty, first for that thou hast created us to thine own image and similitude, but chiefly that thou hast delivered us from that everlasting death and damnation into the which Satan drew mankind by the mean[s] of sin: from the bondage whereof neither man nor angel was able to make us free; but thou, O Lord, rich in mercy and infinite in goodness, hast provided our redemption to stand in thy only and well-beloved Son whom of very love thou didst give to be made man, like unto us in all things (sin except[ed]), that in his body he might receive the punishments of our transgression, by his death to make satisfaction to thy justice, and by his resurrection to destroy him that was author of death, and so to reduce and bring again life to the world, from which the whole offspring of Adam most justly was exiled.

O Lord, we acknowledge that no creature is able to comprehend the length and breadth, the deepness and height, of that thy most excellent love which moved thee to show mercy, where none was deserved; to promise and give life, where death had gotten victory; to receive us into thy grace, when we could do nothing but rebel against thy justice.

O Lord, the blind dullness of our corrupt nature will not suffer us sufficiently to weigh these thy most ample benefits, yet nevertheless at the commandment of Jesus Christ our Lord, we present ourselves to this his table, which he hath left to be used in remembrance of his death until his coming again, to declare and witness before the world, that by him alone we have received liberty and life; that by him alone we have entrance to the throne of thy grace; that by him alone we are possessed in our spiritual kingdom, to eat and drink at his table with whom we have our conversation presently in heaven, and by whom our bodies shall be raised up again from the dust and shall be placed with him in that endless joy, which thou, O father of mercy, hast prepared for thine elect before the foundation of the world was laid.

And these most inestimable benefits we acknowledge and confess to have received of thy free mercy and grace, by thy only beloved Son Jesus Christ, for the which therefore we thy congregation, moved by thy Holy Spirit, render thee all thanks, praise, and glory for ever and ever.

This done, the minister breaketh the bread and delivereth it to the people, who distribute and divide it among themselves, according to our savior Christ's commandment, and in like wise giveth the cup.[15]

Calvin's prayer at Geneva concluded the intercessions of the Sunday preaching service and came before the reading of the warrant and the exhortation. It is not easy to think of it as the table grace for the Lord's Supper. By moving the prayer to a place after the exhortation, Knox subtly changed the character of the celebration. As the first action of the minister when he moved to the table, it marked the true beginning of the celebration of the Lord's Supper and set the tone for the rite—a markedly more positive tone than we find in the Genevan rite. Knox's prayer is not dissimilar in character from some of the very early eucharistic prayers of which we took note above, although it was not introduced by the traditional dialogue.

A distinctive feature of Knox's usage, both in exile in Frankfort and in Scotland, was the custom of seating all communicants (and not just the ministers) at the table. This gave concrete expression to the corporate character of the celebration. Another feature of developing Scottish usage (not reflected in the rubrics of Knox's rite) was a second recitation of the institution narrative by the minister—with necessary changes in the pronouns—as he broke the bread and distributed the bread and wine after the eucharistic prayer.[16] A final characteristic of developing Scottish usage should be noted. Many Scottish ministers felt the lack of an invocation of the Spirit (such as Cranmer's 1549 rite included) and supplied that lack in their own observance of the Lord's Supper.[17]

The Book of Common Order remained in usage in Scotland until it was replaced by the Westminster *Directory for the Public Worship of God throughout the Three Kingdoms of England, Scotland, and Ireland* in 1645. While the Directory provided a set of rubrics rather than the text of a liturgy for the eucharist, it set forth directions for a service which supplied the elements that many felt were lacking in the Book of Common Order. This is the relevant portion of that rite:

> *After this exhortation, warning, and invitation, the Table being before decently covered, and so conveniently placed, that the communicants may orderly sit about it, or at it, the minister is to begin the action with sanctifying and blessing the elements of bread and wine set before him (the bread in comely and convenient vessels, so prepared that, being broken by him, and given, it may be distributed among the communicants; the wine also in large cups), having first, in a few words, showed that these elements, otherwise common, are now set apart and sanctified to this holy use, by the Word of Institution and prayer.*
>
> *Let the Words of Institution be read out of the Evangelists, or out of the first Epistle of the Apostle Paul to the Corinthians, chapter 11:23..., which the minister may, when he seeth requisite, explain and apply.*
>
> *Let the prayer, thanksgiving, or blessing of the bread and wine, be to this effect:*
>
> With humble and hearty acknowledgement of the greatness of our misery, from which neither man nor angel was able to deliver us, and of our great unworthiness of the least of all God's mercies: to give thanks to God for all his benefits, and especially for that benefit of our redemption, the love of God the Father, the suffering and

merits of the Lord Jesus Christ the Son of God, by which we are delivered; and for all the means of grace, the Word and sacraments; and for this sacrament in particular, by which Christ, and all his benefits, are applied and sealed unto us, which, not withstanding the denial of them unto others, are in great mercy continued unto us, after so much and long abuse of them.

To profess that there is no other name under heaven by which we can be saved, but the name of Jesus Christ, by whom alone we receive liberty and life, have access to the throne of grace, are admitted to eat and drink at his own table, and are sealed by his Spirit to an assurance of happiness and everlasting life.

Earnestly to pray to God, the Father of all mercies, and God of all consolation, to vouchsafe his gracious presence, and the effectual working of his Spirit in us; and so to sanctify these elements, both of bread and wine, and to bless his own ordinance, that we may receive by faith the body and blood of Jesus Christ, crucified for us, and so to feed upon him, that he may be one with us, and we with him; that he may live in us, and we in him, and to him who hath loved us, and given himself for us.

All the which he is to endeavor to perform with suitable affections, answerable to such an holy action, and to stir up the like in the people. The elements being now sanctified by the Word and prayer, the minister, being at the table, is to take the bread into his hand and say, in these expressions (or the like, used by Christ or his apostle upon this occasion):

According to the holy institution, command, and example of our blessed Savior Jesus Christ, I take this bread, and having given thanks, I break it, and give it unto you.

Then the minister, who is also himself to communicate, is to break the bread, and give it to the communicants.

Take ye, eat ye; this is the body of Christ, which is broken for you: do this in remembrance of him.

In the like manner the minister is to take the cup, and say, in these expressions (or any other like, used by Christ or the apostle upon the same occasion):

According to the institution, command, and example of our Lord Jesus Christ, I take this cup, and give it unto you.

Here he giveth it to the communicants.

This cup is the New Testament in the blood of Christ, which is shed for the remission of the sins of many: drink ye all of it.

Here at last the Reformed tradition found a rite that gave adequate expression to its eucharistic theology. The line of that tradition which ran from Calvin to Knox to the Westminister Directory, however, intentionally rejected traditional liturgical forms. In a characteristic way the service lacks the dialogical character of liturgical prayer and is a didactic monologue. The true liturgical expression of Reformed eucharistic theology was to be found in a place where few today would expect it—in the Book of Common Prayer of the Church of England.

NOTES

[1] See the treatment of the eucharistic theology of Zwingli in William R. Crockett, *Eucharist: Symbol of Transformation* (New York: Pueblo, 1989), pages 135-145.

[2] Ulrich Zwingli, *Exposition of the Faith* (1523), in G. W. Bromily, ed., *Zwingli and Bullinger: Selected Translations with Introduction and Notes*, page 263.

[3] Ibid, page 264.

[4] For Calvin's eucharistic theology, see Crockett, *Eucharist: Symbol of Transformation*, chapter 5.

[5] John Calvin, *Institutes of the Christian Religion,* Ford Lewis Battles trans. (Philadelphia: Westminster Press, 1955), Book 4, chapter 17, §10, in vol. 2, pages 1370-1371.

[6] John Calvin, *Short Treatise on the Holy Supper of our Lord and only Saviour Jesus Christ*, in J. K. S. Reid, trans., *Calvin: Theological Treatises* (Philadelphia: Westminster Press, n.d.), page 148.

[7] John Calvin, *Institutes*, Book 4, chapter 18, §10, vol. 2, page 1458.

[8] Ibid., § 11, page 1459.

[9] Ibid., § 16, page 1444.

[10] Ibid.

[11] Ibid., page 1445.

[12] Ibid., Book 4, chapter 17, § 46, page 1424. So also in his *Articles concerning the Organization of the Church and of Worship at Geneva proposed by the Ministers in Council, January 16, 1537,* in *Calvin: Theological Treatises*, Calvin declares (page 49): "It would be well to require that the Communion of the Holy Supper of Jesus Christ be held every Sunday at the least as a rule." He did not achieve his goal: in Geneva, the sacrament was celebrated once a quarter in each parish,

with the schedule so organized that it would be celebrated once each month at some church in the city.

[13] *Institutes,* Book 4, chapter 17, § 43, pages 1421-1422.

[14] Translation from Bard Thompson, ed., *Liturgies of the Western Church* (Cleveland and New York: World, 1961), pages 203-207. The text given there presents the rites of Strasbourg (1545) and Geneva (1542). I have given only the Genevan text and reorganized it accordingly.

[15] Text, ibid., pages 303-304. I have modernized the spelling and the punctuation.

[16] See the introduction to Knox's rite in Jasper and Cuming, *Prayers of the Eucharist*, page 252. Note that the next rite which we will consider, that of the Westminister Directory, prescribed such a usage.

[17] See the commentary in W. Jardine Grisbrooke, *Anglican Liturgies of the Seventeenth and Eighteenth Centuries* (London: SPCK, 1958), page 6.

CHAPTER SEVEN

THE TWO STRANDS OF THE ANGLICAN LITURGICAL TRADITION

❖ ❖ ❖ ❖ ❖ ❖ ❖ ❖ ❖ ❖ ❖ ❖ ❖

The EUCHARISTIC PRAYER OF THE 1549 BOOK OF COMMON PRAYER

The first concrete reform of the eucharist in England came in 1547, the first year of the reign of Edward VI, when royal injunctions required that the epistle and gospel be read in English at high mass and a book of homilies was issued for the use of preachers. In 1548 Archbishop Thomas Cranmer issued an order for the administration of communion which was to be inserted into the Latin mass after the celebrant made his communion. This included an exhortation, a penitential order, a prayer of humble access, words of administration, and an English blessing to conclude the service. In 1549 the Church of England adopted a complete Book of Common Prayer, which included daily services, the eucharist for Sundays and feast days, pastoral offices, and (when the ordinal was appended the following year) rites reserved to the bishop.

The character of this first Book of Common Prayer is deceptive. Cranmer retained the structural components of the Latin mass, as Luther had in 1523. But unlike Luther, he retained a complete eucharistic prayer. This prayer is in large part a skillful English paraphrase of the Roman canon, with all the intercessions located after the Sanctus. An outline of its components (with incipits for sections of both the Roman canon and the 1549 rite) will reveal the structural similarity. In the intercessions, I have numbered sections of the Roman canon to indicate their original sequence and listed the paragraphs of the 1549 Prayer by topics.

Roman Canon	1549 Eucharistic Prayer
Eucharistic Dialogue	Eucharistic Dialogue
Preface (with proper prefaces)	Preface (with proper prefaces)
Sanctus/Benedictus	Sanctus/Benedictus
	Prayer for the Whole State of Christ's Church
1. Te igitur (church, clergy, rulers)	for the church
	for king and council
	for bishops and other ministers
	for all members of the church
4. Hanc igitur oblationem	for those in need
2. Memento, Domine	for those gathered for the eucharist
3. Communicantes	for the saints
[Memento etiam]	for the departed
Quam oblationem	O God, heavenly Father…
Qui pridie	Who in the same night…
Unde et memores	Wherefore, O Lord and heavenly Father…
Supra quae/Supplices	And here we offer…
5. Memento etiam/Nobis quoque	And although we be unworthy…
Per quem haec omnia/Per ipsum	by whom, and with whom…

We should note that in the late middle ages, the dialogue, preface, and Sanctus were not understood as part of the eucharistic prayer, and intermediate terminations in the prayer ("through Christ our Lord") gave the impression that the canon was a series of prayers rather than a single prayer. Cranmer's eucharistic prayer is likewise printed as a series of prayers (separated by spaces in the outline above):

1. The Dialogue/Preface/Sanctus;
2. The Prayer for the Whole State of Christ's Church (named for its bidding);
3. The Prayer of Consecration (as it was termed in later Prayer Books);
4. The Prayer of Oblation (as it was later termed).

All subsequent Prayer Books rearrange the four sections of the 1549

Eucharistic Prayer. The way in which the sections were rearranged defined the two strands of the later Anglican eucharistic tradition.

The following is the text of this prayer in 1549. Spelling and punctuation has been modernized and paragraph divisions introduced. I have also included in brackets names given later to the sections of this prayer as well as the material used in the administration of communion.

[Dialogue, Preface, and Sanctus]

V. The Lord be with you.
R. And with thy spirit.
V. Lift up your hearts.
R. We lift them up unto the Lord.
V. Let us give thanks unto our Lord God.
R. It is meet and right so to do.

It is very meet, right, and our bounden duty, that we should at all times and in all places give thanks unto thee, O Lord, holy Father, almighty, everlasting God.

A proper preface may follow.

Therefore with Angels and Archangels and with all the company of heaven, we laud and magnify thy glorious name, evermore praising thee and saying:

> Holy, holy, holy, Lord God of hosts: Heaven
> and earth are full of thy glory. Hosanna in the
> highest. Blessed is he that cometh in the name
> of the Lord. Glory to thee, O Lord, in the
> highest.

[Prayer for the Whole State of Christ's Church]

Let us pray for the whole state of Christ's Church: Almighty and everliving God, which by thy holy Apostle hast taught us to make prayers and supplications, and to give thanks for all men: We humbly beseech thee most mercifully to receive these our prayers, which we offer unto thy divine Majesty, beseeching thee to inspire continually the universal church with the spirit of truth, unity, and concord. And grant that all they that do confess thy holy name may agree in the truth of thy holy word and live in unity and godly love.

Especially we beseech thee to save and defend thy servant N. our King, that under him we may be godly and quietly governed. And grant unto his whole council and to all that be put in authority under him that they may truly and indifferently minister justice, to the punishment of wickedness and vice and to the maintenance of thy true religion and virtue.

Give grace, O heavenly Father, to all bishops, pastors, and curates, that they may both by their life and doctrine set forth thy true and lively word and rightly and duly administer thy holy Sacraments.

And to all thy people give thy heavenly grace, that with meek heart and true reverence they may hear and receive thy holy word, truly serving thee in holiness and righteousness all the days of their life.

And we most humbly beseech thee of thy goodness, O Lord, to comfort and succor all them which in this transitory life be in trouble, sorrow, need, sickness, or any other adversity.

And especially we commend unto thy merciful goodness this congregation which is here assembled in thy name to celebrate the commemoration of the most glorious death of thy Son.

And here we do yield thee most high praise and hearty thanks for the wonderful grace and virtue declared in all thy saints from the beginning of the world: and chiefly in the glorious and most blessed virgin Mary, mother of thy Son Jesu Christ, our Lord and God, and in thy holy patriarchs, prophets, apostles, and martyrs, whose examples, O Lord, and steadfastness in the faith and keeping thy commandments grant us to follow.

We commend unto thy mercy, O Lord, all other thy servants which are departed hence from us with the sign of faith and now do rest in the sleep of peace: Grant unto them, we beseech thee, thy mercy and everlasting peace, and that, at the day of the general resurrection, we and all they that be of the mystical body of thy Son may all together be set on his right hand and hear that his most blessed voice: Come unto me, O ye that be blessed of my Father, and possess the kingdom which is prepared for you from the beginning of the world. Grant this, O Father, for Jesus Christ's sake, our only Mediator and Advocate.

[Prayer of Consecration]

O God, heavenly Father, which of thy tender mercy didst give thine only Son Jesus Christ to suffer death upon the cross for our redemption, who made there, by his one oblation of himself once offered, a full, perfect, and sufficient sacrifice, oblation, and satisfaction for the sins of the whole world and did institute and in his holy Gospel command us to continue a perpetual memory of that his precious death and sacrifice until his coming again: Hear us, O merciful Father, we beseech thee, and with thy Holy Spirit and word vouchsafe to bl+ess and sanc+tify these thy gifts and creatures of bread and wine, that they may be unto us the body and blood of thy most dearly beloved Son Jesus Christ:

Who in the same night that he was betrayed took bread, and when he had blessed and given thanks he brake it and gave it to his disciples, saying: Take, eat: this is my body which is given for you. Do this in remembrance of me. Likewise after supper he took the cup, and when he had given thanks he gave it to them, saying: Drink, ye all, of this: for this is my blood of the New Testament which is shed for you and for many for the remission of sins. Do this, as oft as ye shall drink it, in remembrance of me.

[Prayer of Oblation]

Wherefore, O Lord and heavenly Father, according to the institution of thy dearly beloved Son, our savior Jesu Christ, we thy humble servants do celebrate and make here before thy divine Majesty, with these thy holy gifts, the memorial which thy Son hath willed us to make, having in remembrance his blessed passion, mighty resurrection, and glorious ascension, rendering unto thee most hearty thanks for the innumerable benefits procured unto us by the same; entirely desiring thy fatherly goodness mercifully to accept this our sacrifice of praise and thanksgiving: most humbly beseeching thee to grant that by the merits and death of thy Son Jesus Christ and through faith in his blood we and all thy whole church may obtain remission of our sins and all other benefits of his passion.

And here we offer and present unto thee, O Lord, ourselves, our souls and bodies, to be a reasonable, holy, and lively sacrifice unto thee: humbly beseeching thee that whosoever shall be partakers of this holy communion may worthily receive the most precious body and blood of thy Son Jesus Christ and be fulfilled with thy grace and heavenly benediction and made one body with thy Son Jesu Christ, that he may dwell in them, and they in him.

And although we be unworthy through our manifold sins to offer unto thee any sacrifice, yet we beseech thee to accept this our bounden duty and service and command these our prayers and supplications, by the ministry of thy holy Angels, to be brought up into thy holy tabernacle before the sight of thy divine Majesty, not weighing our merits, but pardoning our offences; through Jesus Christ our Lord: by whom and with whom, in the unity of the Holy Ghost, all honor and glory be unto thee, O Father almighty, world without end. Amen.

[Lord's Prayer]

[Peace]

[Invitation]

Christ our Paschal Lamb is offered up for us once for all, when he bare our sins on his body upon the cross, for he is the very lamb of God that taketh away the sins of the world: wherefore let us keep a joyful and holy feast with the Lord.

[Invitation, Confession, Absolution, Comfortable Words]

[Anthem during the Administration of Communion]

O lamb of God, that taketh away the sins of the world, have mercy upon us.

O lamb of God, that taketh away the sins of the world, have mercy upon us.

O lamb of God, that taketh away the sins of the world, grant us thy peace.

[Administration of Communion]

The body of our Lord Jesus Christ which was given for thee preserve thy body and soul unto everlasting life.

The blood of our Lord Jesus Christ which was shed for thee preserve thy body and soul unto everlasting life.[1]

We should note several features of this prayer. First of all, from the eucharistic dialogue through the Sanctus, Cranmer has provided a free translation of the equivalent texts of the Roman canon. From that point on, Cranmer follows the thematic sequence of the canon, but the text is his own composition. He has collected the intercessions of the canon into a single prayer, drawing on the work of the Reformed liturgist Martin Bucer and others rather than working with the Roman text. For the Quam oblationem, which functions in the Roman canon as a petition for consecration, he has substituted a petition that God bless and sanctify the gifts with his Holy Spirit and word (an invocation). He may have drawn on his knowledge of Eastern liturgies in crafting this petition. The Roman canon has an anamnesis with an oblation of the bread and wine after the institution narrative. Cranmer has in its place an anamnesis with a petition for the acceptance of the church's sacrifice of praise and thanksgiving (like the anamnesis/thanksgiving of the anaphora of the apostles). The Roman petition for the acceptance of the oblation of bread and wine (Supra quae/Supplices) becomes an act of self-oblation. The plea that God would receive our sacrifice at the hand of an angel becomes a plea that God would receive our prayers and supplications at the hand of the angels and is incorporated into Cranmer's paraphrase of the Nobis quoque.

Cranmer has skillfully reworked the material of the canon to embody the Reformed doctrine of the eucharistic sacrifice. A careful reading of Cranmer's text reveals that the sacrifice offered to God is a sacrifice of praise and thanksgiving, but that this sacrifice is not associated with the bread and wine (as in the Roman canon and in most classical anaphoras) but with the self-oblation of the communicants. And whereas in the Roman canon and in most of the classical anaphoras the bread and wine offered are understood as figures of Christ's body and blood, so that the church's oblation is united with Christ's sacrifice, no such association is made here. The text of the prayer sets out the meaning of eucharistic sacrifice as Calvin expounds it in his Institutes, giving it liturgical expression in a way that none of the other Reformed rites had done. In the introductory section of the prayer of consecration and in the anthem after the peace, Cranmer makes clear that Christ's sacrifice was offered once upon the cross. We might note in closing that, while the text of the Roman canon does suggest that the church's sacrifice is united with Christ's sacrifice, it does not actually suggest that the church offers Christ in sacrifice at the eucharist. The doctrine which the Reformers repudiated was not implicit in the text of the Roman canon.

The issue of eucharistic presence is more complex. Cranmer's petition for the consecration of the gifts gives liturgical expression to Calvin's understanding of the role of the Holy Spirit at the eucharist. It is as strong a petition—but also as ambiguous a petition—as that found in the Roman canon. Both the Roman canon and the 1549 prayer ask that the bread and wine may be "to us" the body and blood of Christ. Medieval theology understood that as a petition for the transubstantiation of the elements. But it is also possible to understand it in other ways. Cranmer himself declared:

> ...in the book of the holy communion, we do not pray absolutely that the bread and wine may be made the body and blood of Christ, but that unto us in that holy mystery they may be so; that is to say, that we may so worthily receive the same, that we may be partakers of Christ's body and blood, and that therewith in spirit and in truth we may be spiritually nourished.[2]

Indeed, since the Roman canon continues to speak of the elements as bread and wine after the petition for their consecration, it might be argued that the doctrine of transubstantiation is inconsistent with the text of the canon also. While Cranmer's 1549 prayer sets forth the Reformed doctrine of eucharistic sacrifice quite explicitly, it does not clearly articulate any specific doctrine of the eucharistic presence. The rubrical prohibition of the elevation of the elements in the traditional place in the course of the institution narrative, however, suggests that Cranmer sought to repudiate the doctrine of transubstantiation.

The Eucharistic Prayer of the 1552 Book of Common Prayer

Cranmer's conservative opponents argued that the 1549 text of the eucharistic prayer set out the doctrine of eucharistic sacrifice and of transubstantiation that he sought to repudiate. Cranmer's prayer carefully sets out the Reformed doctrine of eucharistic sacrifice, so that this argument is a misreading of the text in that regard. But since the petition for consecration is as strongly worded and as ambiguous as that in the Roman canon, his opponents could make a reasonable case in regard to the eucharistic presence.

There are indications that from the beginning Cranmer meant the 1549 rite to be the first step in the reform of worship in the Church of England, not the final act. What he had skillfully done was to recast the traditional form of worship so that it embodied Reformed doctrine while maintaining a large measure of liturgical continuity. But the interpretation of the eucharist by his conservative opponents and the distaste of many of his Reformed colleagues for the rite incited him to a much more radical treatment of the eucharistic prayer in the 1552 Book of Common Prayer. Every part of the 1549 rite that his conservative opponents cited to support their position on eucharistic sacrifice and presence was recast in 1552 to exclude such an interpretation.

Let us look at how Cranmer refashioned the 1549 eucharistic prayer in 1552. He first of all removed the intercessions (the Prayer for the Whole State of Christ's Church) from the eucharistic prayer and placed them after the sermon, at the conclusion of what we would call the liturgy of the word. He replaced them with what we know as the prayer of humble access. In what would later be called the prayer of consecration, he replaced the petition for the consecration of the gifts (the invocation) with a prayer that those who received the bread and wine might be partakers of Christ's body and blood. He also incorporated into this petition elements of the anamnesis of his prayer of oblation. Communion came immediately after the institution narrative. The last section of his eucharistic prayer, the prayer of oblation, was made an alternative postcommunion prayer. From this prayer Cranmer removed the anamnesis and also the petition that an angel might present the prayer of the church in God's presence in heaven. This prayer thus served to interpret the thankful self-oblation of those who had been united with Christ through communion. Let us look at the resulting text:

[Dialogue, Preface, Sanctus]

V. Lift up your hearts.
R. We lift them up unto the Lord.
V. Let us give thanks unto our Lord God.
R. It is meet and right so to do.

It is very meet, right, and our bounden duty, that we should at all times and in all places give thanks unto thee, O Lord, holy Father, almighty, everlasting God.

A proper preface may follow.

Therefore with Angels and Archangels and with all the company of heaven, we laud and magnify thy glorious name, evermore praising thee and saying:

Holy, holy, holy, Lord God of hosts: Heaven and earth are full of thy glory. Glory be to thee, O Lord most high.

[Prayer of Humble Access]

We do not presume to come to this thy table, O merciful Lord, trusting in our own righteousness, but in thy manifold and great mercies. We be not worthy so much as to gather up the crumbs under thy table. But thou art the same Lord whose property is always to have mercy. Grant us therefore, gracious Lord, so to eat the flesh of thy dear Son Jesus Christ and to drink his blood, that our sinful bodies may be made clean by his body and our souls washed by his most precious blood, and that we may evermore dwell in him, and he in us. Amen.

[Prayer of Consecration]

Almighty God, our heavenly Father, which of thy tender mercy didst give thine only Son Jesus Christ to suffer death upon the cross for our redemption, who made there, by his one oblation of himself once offered, a full, perfect, and sufficient sacrifice, oblation, and satisfaction for the sins of the whole world and did institute and in his holy Gospel command us to continue a perpetual memory of that his precious death until his coming again: Hear us, O merciful Father, we beseech thee, and grant that we, receiving these thy creatures of bread and wine, according to thy Son our Savior Jesus Christ's holy institution, in remembrance of his death and passion, may be partakers of his most blessed body and blood:

Who in the same night that he was betrayed took bread, and when he had given thanks he brake it and gave it to his disciples, saying: Take, eat: this is my body which is given for you. Do this in remembrance of me. Likewise after supper he took the cup, and when he had given thanks he gave it to them, saying: Drink, ye all, of this: for this is my blood of the New Testament which is shed for you and for many for the remission of sins. Do this, as oft as ye shall drink it, in remembrance of me.

[Administration of Communion]

Take and eat this in remembrance that Christ died for thee, and feed on him in thy heart by faith, with thanksgiving.

Drink this in remembrance that Christ's blood was shed for thee, and be thankful.

[Lord's Prayer]

[Prayer of Oblation as Alternative Postcommunion Prayer]

O Lord and heavenly Father, we thy humble servants entirely desire thy fatherly goodness mercifully to accept this our sacrifice of praise and thanksgiving: most humbly beseeching thee to grant that by the merits and death of thy Son Jesus Christ and through faith in his blood we and all thy whole church may obtain remission of our sins and all other benefits of his passion.

And here we offer and present unto thee, O Lord, ourselves, our souls and bodies, to be a reasonable, holy, and lively sacrifice unto thee: humbly beseeching thee that all we which be partakers of this holy communion may be fulfilled with thy grace and heavenly benediction.

And although we be unworthy through our manifold sins to offer unto thee any sacrifice, yet we beseech thee to accept this our bounden duty and service, not weighing our merits, but pardoning our offences; through Jesus Christ our Lord: by whom and with whom, in the unity of the Holy Ghost, all honor and glory be unto thee, O Father almighty, world without end. Amen.[3]

Unlike the Book of 1549, this book had no rubrics for manual actions during the preparation of the bread and wine, during the institution narrative, or at the fraction. This text remained in use until Queen Mary restored the Roman rite during her reign. After her death, her successor Queen Elizabeth restored the 1552 rite with slight modifications in 1559. The most important of these was the fusion of the 1549 words of administration with the 1552 words. Slight modifications (largely rubrical) were made in later editions of the Prayer Book (manual actions were restored in 1662), but the text has survived until the present day in the Church of England and is the basic text for the English strand of eucharistic prayers in the Anglican tradition. An important rubric was inserted by order of council in the 1552 book, but removed in 1559. It was restored in 1662 with slight but significant variations in wording. This is the famous Black Rubric about the presence of Christ. The two texts are as follows:

1552 Text	1662 Text
Lest yet the same kneeling might be thought or taken otherwise, we do declare that it is not meant thereby, that any adoration is done, or ought to be done, either unto the sacramental bread or wine there bodily received, or unto any *real or essential* presence there being of Christ's natural body and blood. For as concerning the sacramental bread and wine, they remain still in their very natural substances, and therefore may not be adored, for that were idolatry to be abhorred by all faithful Christians. And as concerning the natural body and blood of our savior Christ, they are in heaven and not here. For it is against the truth of Christ's body to be in more places than in one at one time.[4]	...yet lest the same kneeling should by any persons, either out of ignorance or infirmity, or out of any malice and obstinacy, be misconstrued and depraved, it is hereby declared that thereby no adoration is done, or ought to be done, either unto the sacramental bread or wine there bodily received, or unto any *corporal* presence of Christ's natural flesh and blood. For the sacramental bread and wine remain still in their very natural substances, and therefore may not be adored, for that were idolatry to be abhorred by all faithful Christians; and the natural body and blood of our savior Christ are in heaven and not here, it being against the truth of Christ's body to be at one time in more places than in one.

It is important to see what is being denied in this rubric in both its forms. What is being denied is the common understanding of the medieval doctrine of transubstantiation. According to that understanding the body and blood of Christ in their natural state are the reality present under the outward appearances of bread and wine. But this is not an accurate understanding of either Thomas Aquinas's definition of the real presence (which is neither local nor corporal) nor that of Luther (for whom the mode of Christ's presence is not natural and it is the *glorified* body and blood which are present). In the 1552 definition, "real presence" means the presence of Christ's body and blood in their natural state as the *res* of the sacrament. Cranmer would not have affirmed the definition of the real presence set out by either Aquinas or Luther, but the rubric itself does not deny the presence in the terms of either definition.

Cranmer's thought about the presence of Christ at the eucharist was fluid,[5] shifting as he read first Ratramnus and then contemporary continental reformers. At one point it appears that he made Zwingli's position his own, but his final position appears close to that of Calvin and Bucer: in communion the faithful communicant becomes a partaker of both the benefits and the substance of Christ's body and blood. But he does not directly associate this presence with the bread and wine. The elements are the instrumental means of participation in Christ's body and blood, but they do not "contain" Christ's body and blood. It was the doctrine that would later be known as receptionism. William R. Crockett sums up Cranmer's approach in this way:

> His doctrine can perhaps best be described as a doctrine of the real partaking of the body and blood of Christ in the eucharist rather than as a doctrine of the real objective presence of Christ in the eucharist. The sacramental signs are connected with the reality that they signify through their use rather than in an objective manner. Such a standpoint represents an attempt to retain sacramental realism in relation to the faithful believer rather than in relation to the elements.[6]

That is certainly the interpretation most easily supported by the text of the liturgy. But the shape of the 1552 rite has moved away from the classical structure of taking, giving thanks, breaking, and sharing. Cranmer has skillfully used prayer to articulate his theology, but he has done so at the cost of abandoning fidelity to the shape that the New Testament suggests for the rite.

Later Anglican Interpretation of the 1552 Rite

Anglicanism has been characterized by fidelity to its liturgical tradition rather than by fidelity to precise theological definitions of the eucharistic presence and the eucharistic sacrifice. But the tradition did develop a classical approach to these issues in the seventeenth century. Our focus here is on the eucharistic prayer itself rather than on eucharistic doctrine, so I will simply cite characteristic treatments of these issues. Anglicans in this period generally affirmed the real presence of Christ at the eucharist. In the sacramental material added to the catechism in the 1604 edition of the Book of Common Prayer, we find the real presence affirmed in the following questions and answers:

> *Question.* What is the outward part or sign of the Lord's Supper?
> *Answer.* Bread and Wine, which the Lord hath commanded to be received.
> *Question.* What is the inward part, or thing signified?
> *Answer.* The Body and Blood of Christ, which are verily and indeed taken and received by the faithful in the Lord's Supper.[7]

A careful reading of the second answer reveals a receptionist perspective: reception by the faithful is part of the definition.

Some Anglican authors, however, were ready to associate the presence more closely with the elements. The best definition of the eucharistic presence from this period is perhaps that of William Nicholson,

Bishop of Gloucester after the Restoration:

> Christ is said to be present in four manner of ways:
>
> 1. Divinely, as God, and so he is present in all places. *Whither shall I fly from Thy presence? I, the Lord, fill heaven and earth.*
>
> 2. Spiritually, and so He is present in the hearts of true believers. *Christ dwells in our hearts by faith.*
>
> 3. Sacramentally, and so He is present in the Sacrament, because He hath ordained the Sacrament to represent and communicate Christ's death unto us. *The cup of blessing which we bless, is it not the communion of the blood of Christ, etc.?*
>
> 4. Corporally; so present in Judaea in the days of his flesh.
>
> And as the word "presence," so the word "really" is diversely taken; for sometimes,
>
> 1. It is opposed to that which is feigned, and is but imaginary, and imports as much as "truly."
>
> 2. It is opposed to that which is merely figurative, and barely representative, and imports as much as "effectually."
>
> 3. It is opposed to that which is spiritual, and imports as much as "corporally" or "bodily."
>
> We then believe Christ to be present in the Eucharist Divinely after a special manner, Spiritually in the hearts of the communicants, Sacramentally or relatively in the elements. And this presence of His is real, in the former two acceptions of "real"; but not in the last, for He is truly and effectually there present, though not corporally, bodily, carnally, locally.[8]

Anglican authors argued that this presence of Christ was effected by the consecration, and indeed later editions of the Prayer Book would designate the text which included the petition for a fruitful communion and the institution narrative "the prayer of consecration." From the perspective of a receptionist view of the eucharistic presence, such a prayer did not "make" the bread and wine the body and blood of Christ, but rather "set them apart" as the sacramental means by which the communicants received the body and blood of Christ. The logic of the later editions of the Prayer Book, which mandated the use of the words of institution to consecrate additional elements if what was consecrated proved insufficient for the number of communicants, is that it was the words of institution that consecrated. Indeed, the wording of the 1549 invocation, which asks God to bless and sanctify the elements by his Holy Spirit and word, probably refers to the words of Christ in the institution narrative (rather than to Christ the Word). Seventeenth century Anglicans, well-read in the Greek fathers and Greek liturgies, would speak of the agency of the Holy Spirit in the consecration of the gifts, but the text of the prayer of consecration no longer provided a basis for this, since the invocation of the Spirit had been removed in 1552.

Some Anglicans in this period would go so far as to speak of the consecration effecting a change in the elements, though they were careful to qualify what they meant by such a change. John Cosin would write:

> ...because this is a Sacrament, the change must be understood to be sacramental also, whereby common Bread and Wine become the Sacrament of the Body and Blood of Christ; which could not be, did not the substance of the Bread and Wine remain, for a Sacrament consisteth in two parts, an earthly and heavenly. And so because ordinary bread is changed by consecration into a bread which is no more of common use...it is therefore said by some of the Fathers to be changed....[9]

Notice that this claim is carefully formulated to deny the doctrine of transubstantiation.

Anglicans at the time of the Reformation were less shy of applying sacrificial language to the eucharist than were Continental reformers. We have already noted the carefully crafted articulation of a Reformed doctrine of the eucharistic sacrifice in liturgical texts of the Book of Common Prayer. This doctrine becomes more pronounced in the seventeenth century. At the Restoration John Bramhall summed up the positive thrust of Anglican doctrine in this way:

> We acknowledge an Eucharistical Sacrifice of praise and thanksgiving; a commemorative Sacrifice or a memorial of the Sacrifice of the cross; a representative Sacrifice, or a representation of the Passion of Christ before the eyes of his heavenly Father; an impetrative Sacrifice, or an impetration of the fruits and benefits of His Passion by way of real prayer; and lastly, an applicative Sacrifice, or an application of his merits unto our souls.[10]

Jeremy Taylor was one of the first to formulate this in terms of the Christology of Hebrews in such a way as to unite the church's sacrifice with the sacrifice which Christ pleaded before his Father in heaven:

> [Christ] exhibits the sacrifice, that is, himself, actually and presentially in heaven; the priest on earth commemorates the same, and, by his prayers, represents it to God in behalf of the whole catholic church, presentially too, by another and more mysterious way of presence; but both Christ in heaven, and his ministers on earth, do actuate the sacrifice, and apply it to its purposed design by praying to God in the virtue and merit of that sacrifice; Christ himself, in a high and glorious manner; the ministers of his priesthood (as it

becomes ministers) humbly, sacramentally, and according to the energy of human advocation and intercession; this is the sum and great mysteriousness of Christianity, and is now to be proved.[11]

A higher doctrinal view of the eucharistic presence, consecration, and eucharistic sacrifice is to be found in the works of John Johnson in the eighteenth century. Johnson and those who followed him developed their doctrine on the basis of the eastern liturgies, and it did not cohere easily with the English rite. It was to find its most adequate expression in that strand of Anglican liturgical tradition which emerged first in the Episcopal Church of Scotland with the abortive Prayer Book of 1637 and then with the eucharistic rite of 1764. It is to this strand of the tradition that we now turn.

THE SCOTTISH PRAYER BOOK OF 1637 AND THE EUCHARISTIC RITE OF 1764

Many Anglican theologians in the seventeenth century gave increasing importance to the role of the Holy Spirit at the eucharist on the basis of Calvin's eucharistic theology and their study of the Greek fathers and Greek liturgies. Of the Greek liturgies, the rite found in Book 8 of the Apostolic Constitutions and the liturgy of St. James enjoyed particular favor. Such study resulted in distinctive doctrines of the eucharistic presence and of eucharistic consecration and gave importance to the oblation of bread and wine in the way that the doctrine of the eucharistic sacrifice was formulated.

The doctrine of the eucharistic presence which developed in this strand of Anglicanism is usually known as virtualism. It is related to Calvin's argument that Christ is present at the eucharist by the virtue (that is, the power) of the Spirit, but it associates that presence more closely to the eucharistic elements than Calvin did. The best expositor of this doctrine (and the related doctrines of consecration and eucharistic sacrifice) is John Johnson, rector of Cranbrook in the early eighteenth century. Johnson wrote:

1. The Body and Blood in the Sacrament are the Bread and Wine.

2. The Body and Blood in the Sacrament, or the Consecrated Bread and Wine, are Types of the Natural Body and Blood of Christ.

3. But they are not such cold and imperfect Types as those before and under the Law.

4. Nay, they are the very Body and Blood, tho' not in Substance, yet in Spirit, Power, and Effect.[12]

His doctrine of consecration is closely related to his doctrine of the presence, and is based on the structure of the West Syrian anaphoras which we explored earlier. He writes

> ...the Holy Ghost was, by the Vote of Antiquity, the principal immediate Cause of the Bread and Wine's becoming the Body and Blood ....
>
> The Subordinate or Mediate Cause of it is, 1. The Reciting of the Words of Institution. 2. The Oblation of the Symbols. 3. The Prayer of Invocation. All these did, in the ancient Liturgies, immediately follow each other, in the order that I have mentioned them; and each of them was believed to contribute toward the Consecration of the Elements into the Body and Blood.[13]

Johnson's doctrine of the eucharistic sacrifice is based upon such a structure for the eucharistic prayer and upon the Christology of Hebrews. He sets it out in the following way, arguing that

> [Christ] did, as a Priest, offer his Body and Blood, in the Eucharist, under the pledges of Bread and Wine; that He was afterwards slain as a Sacrifice on the Cross.... He finish'd the Sacrifice of Himself by entering as a High-Priest into Heaven, the true Holy of Holies, and He gives life to our Sacrifice, by always appearing there in the Presence of God for us.[14]

From this perspective, the oblation of the bread and wine are a key part of the eucharistic sacrifice, for it is the offering of these elements as antitypes or figures of the body and blood of Christ that unites the church's eucharistic sacrifice with the one sacrifice that Christ pleads before the heavenly altar. Johnson writes:

> When we say, we offer Bread and Wine, we don't only mean the Products and First-fruits of the Earth; but the Memorials of Christ's Passion, the Authoritative Representations of Christ's Body and Blood; or, if you will speak with the primitive Church, the true Body and Blood of Christ....[15]

It is apparent that this strand of Anglican eucharistic theology did not easily fit with the Prayer Book of 1559, which was more in accord with a receptionist view of the eucharistic presence and a doctrine of sacrifice which focussed on the eucharist as a commemorative sacrifice and on the communicants' self-oblation as a sacrifice of praise and thanksgiving. It was much easier to reconcile with the 1549 rite, which attached the prayer of oblation to the prayer of consecration and which included an invocation of the Spirit upon the elements rather than a petition for fruitful communion. The 1549 rite did not have the structural sequence of the West Syrian prayers that Johnson had identified, but it did have the components which he picked out in those prayers. It did not include an explicit oblation of the bread and wine, but the preparation of the elements at the offertory could be interpreted as an oblation (though that was not Cranmer's intention). Those who followed this strand of eucharistic doctrine generally favored a restoration of the 1549 rite, but even in 1662 the political climate did not make such a restoration possible.

It was the Church of Scotland, not the Church of England, which moved in the direction suggested by this eucharistic theology. This Church adopted a presbyterian polity and Knox's eucharistic liturgy at the Reformation settlement of 1560. But when James VI of Scotland ascended to the throne of the United Kingdom in 1601, he superimposed bishops upon the Church of Scotland, and his successor, Charles I, sought to introduce the Prayer Book in Scotland as well. The bishops of the Scottish Church, however, produced an edition of the Prayer Book in 1637 for use in Scotland that restored to the eucharist a large part of the 1549 structure. We might outline the eucharistic prayer and related materials in that rite as follows:

[Offertory Rubric]

And when all have offered, [the Deacon or one of the Churchwardens] shall reverently bring the said bason with the oblations therein, and deliver it to the Presbyter, who shall humbly present it before the Lord, and set it upon the holy Table. And the Presbyter shall then offer up and place the bread and wine prepared for the Sacrament upon the Lord's Table, that it may be ready for that service.

[Prayer for the Whole State of Christ's Church]

[Exhortations, Invitation, Confession, Absolution, Comfortable Words]

[Dialogue, Preface, Sanctus]

["Prayer of Consecration" (invocation restored); rubrics for manual acts]

["Memorial or Prayer of Oblation"]

[Lord's Prayer]

["Collect of Humble Access"]

[Communion: 1549 words of administration]

Although the intercessions were not reincorporated into the eucharistic prayer, its structure otherwise conformed to that of 1549. We should note two small textual variants and two significant ones. First, the prayer of consecration expands the phrase "a perpetual memory of that his precious death" into "a perpetual memory of that his precious death and sacrifice," thus explicitly describing the eucharist as a memorial of Christ's sacrifice. Second, the reference to the agency of angels in presenting our prayers to God was not restored to the end of the Prayer of Oblation. But the anamnesis at the beginning of this prayer was restored. The explicit invocation of the Holy Spirit was also restored to the Prayer of Consecration, combining the 1549 wording with that of 1552 as follows:

> Hear us, O merciful Father, we most humbly beseech thee, and of thy almighty goodness vouchsafe to bless and sanctify with thy word and Holy Spirit these thy gifts and creatures of bread and wine, that they may be unto us the body and blood of thy most dearly beloved Son; so that we, receiving them according to thy Son Jesus Christ's holy institution, in remembrance of his death and passion, may be partakers of the same his most precious body and blood.[16]

This book actually incorporated many features of Scottish worship not found in the English Book of Common Prayer at that time—directions for the preparation of the bread and wine, manual acts, an explicit invocation of the Spirit. But it was a book imposed by episcopal authority in a country where the royal imposition of bishops on the church had not been popular and where more radical Puritans sought to abandon any fixed text for a liturgy. It met with such opposition that it was soon withdrawn. The Scots would soon abolish the episcopate as well.

With the restoration of the monarchy after the Commonwealth the episcopate was also restored to the Scottish Church, but no attempt was made to reimpose the Prayer Book. After the Revolution of 1688 the Church of Scotland reverted to a Presbyterian polity when none of its bishops would take the oath of allegiance to William and Mary. These "non-juring" bishops and clergy associated with them eventually formed themselves into the Episcopal Church of Scotland. When in the eighteenth century they determined to adopt a fixed liturgy once more, they did not adopt the English Book of Common Prayer but eventually went back to the eucharistic rite of 1637. But their study of Eastern liturgies left them unsatisfied with that book as well, and they began to rearrange its structure to conform to the pattern set out early in the century by John Johnson. This form of the eucharist became the official liturgy in 1764. This is the text of those parts of it that are pertinent to our study of the eucharistic prayer:

[At the Offertory]

And the Presbyter shall then offer up, and place the bread and wine prepared for the sacrament upon the Lord's table....

[Dialogue, Preface, and Sanctus]

["The Prayer of Consecration"]

ALL glory be to thee, Almighty God, our heavenly Father, for that thou of thy tender mercy didst give thy only Son Jesus Christ to suffer death upon the cross for our redemption; who (by his own oblation of himself once offered) made a full, perfect, and sufficient sacrifice, oblation, and satisfaction, for the sins of the whole world, and did institute, and in his holy gospel command us to continue a perpetual memorial of that his precious death and sacrifice until his coming again.

For in the night that he was betrayed, he took bread; and when he had given thanks, he brake it, and gave it to his disciples, saying, Take, eat, THIS IS MY BODY, which is given for you: Do this in remembrance of me. Likewise after supper he took the cup; and when he had given thanks, he gave it to them, saying, Drink ye all of this, for THIS IS MY BLOOD of the new testament, which is shed for you and for many, for the remission of sins. Do this as oft as ye shall drink it in remembrance of me.

["The Oblation"]

WHEREFORE, O Lord and heavenly Father, according to the institution of thy dearly beloved Son our Saviour Jesus Christ, we thy humble servants do celebrate and make here before thy divine majesty, with these thy holy gifts, WHICH WE NOW OFFER UNTO THEE, the memorial thy son hath commanded us to make; having in remembrance his blessed passion, and precious death, his mighty resurrection, and glorious ascension; rendering unto thee most hearty thanks for the innumerable benefits procured unto us by the same.

["The Invocation"]

And we most humbly beseech thee, O merciful Father, to hear us, and of thy almighty goodness vouchsafe to bless and sanctify, with thy word and Holy Spirit, these thy gifts and creatures of bread and wine, that they may become the body and blood of thy most dearly beloved Son.

And we earnestly desire thy fatherly goodness, mercifully to accept this our sacrifice of praise and thanksgiving, most humbly beseeching thee to grant, that by the merits and death of thy Son Jesus Christ, and through faith in his blood, we (and all thy whole church) may obtain remission of our sins, and all other benefits of his passion.

And here we humbly offer and present unto thee, O Lord, ourselves, our souls and bodies, to be a reasonable, holy, and lively sacrifice unto thee, beseeching thee, that whosoever shall be partakers of this holy Communion, may worthily receive the most precious body and blood of thy Son Jesus Christ, and be filled with thy grace and heavenly benediction, and made one body with him, that he may dwell in them, and they in him.

And although we are unworthy, through our manifold sins, to offer unto thee any sacrifice; yet we beseech thee to accept this our bounden duty and service, not weighing our merits, but pardoning our offences, through Jesus [Christ] our Lord: by whom, and with whom, in the unity of the Holy Ghost, all honour and glory be unto thee, O Father Almighty, world without end. Amen.

[Prayer for the Whole State of Christ's Church]

[Lord's Prayer]

[Invitation, Confession, Absolution, Comfortable Words]

[Collect of Humble Access]

[Administration of Communion: 1549 Words][17]

In this rite the Scottish bishops took their 1637 communion office and rearranged its components to fit the structure of the West Syrian anaphoras. Particularly important was the liturgy of St. James, which Thomas Rattray, Scottish primus at the beginning of the eighteenth century, considered "the ancient liturgy of the Church of Jerusalem." But the influence of John Johnson is also apparent, as we shall see in analyzing the changes. Not only does the eucharistic prayer move the invocation of the Spirit to its West Syrian place in the anaphora, it also moves the anaphoral intercessions (the Prayer for the Whole State of Christ's Church) to the end of the prayer. There are also other small but significant changes in the 1637 eucharistic prayer besides the rearrangement of the text. The wording of the invocation does not, as in 1637, conflate the 1549 text with the 1552 petition for a fruitful communion, but follows the 1549 wording closely—and even omits the "to us," which might be read in a receptionist way. The anamnesis was expanded with an explicit oblation of the elements, printed in upper case letters in the text of the rite. In 1637 there was a rubrical oblation of the elements at the offertory; now there was an explicit oblation as well, at the place in the eucharistic prayer where that oblation occurs in Eastern liturgies. The specific oblation of the elements is a concrete expression of the unity of the church's sacrifice with the sacrifice of

Christ: the bread and wine are both tokens of our sacrifice of praise and thanksgiving and antitypes of Christ's sole sufficient sacrifice for the sins of the world.

We should finally note two changes in the introduction to the institution narrative. With the removal of the invocation from the Prayer of Consecration, the remainder of the introduction was a dangling sentence fragment. The Scots reworded the opening of the introduction, adding the phrase "All glory be to thee" and thus linking it to the Sanctus. This is an Anglican link: as we have seen, the standard West Syrian link uses the word "Holy," while the Alexandrian link uses the word "Full." The wording of another phrase in the introduction was also altered: "by his one oblation of himself once offered" became "by his own oblation once offered"—conforming to Johnson's understanding of Christ's sacrifice as offered at the last supper, completed on the cross, and presented at the heavenly altar after his ascension.

The new link between the Sanctus and the post-Sanctus in this prayer moves the institution narrative and the anamnesis into the thanksgiving section of the prayer in a very skillful way. But in other ways the Scottish prayer reflects the Western rather than the West Syrian tradition, for it retains a series of proper prefaces rather than a fixed preface that covers the whole scope of God's work in creation and redemption. We also see here an extraordinary use of a text that is Eastern in its inspiration to articulate a eucharistic theology that is Calvinist in origin. What makes this possible is the importance in both Eastern and Calvinist traditions of the role of the Spirit in making Christ present to the communicant and in sealing the benefits of Christ's sacrifice to the communicant.

The Scottish communion office stands at the beginning of a second strand of the Anglican liturgical tradition. A modified form of its eucharistic prayer (without the Prayer for the Whole State of Christ's Church) was adopted by the American Episcopal Church in 1789 and placed within the framework of the English rite of 1662. At the beginning of the twentieth century this strand of the Anglican tradition commended itself to many of the churches that were revising their Prayer Books and desired to restore a full eucharistic prayer. In the late twentieth century revisions, it provided the structural framework for most of the new eucharistic prayers in the Anglican communion (though many kept the invocation in its 1549 rather than its 1764 position).

NOTES

[1] Text from *The First and Second Prayer Books of Edward VI* (London: J. M. Dent & Sons, and New York: E. P. Dutton, 1910), pages 219-225.

[2] Thomas Cranmer, *Works* (Parker Society Edition), vol. 1, page 79.

[3] *The First and Second Prayer Books of Edward VI*, pages 387-390. I have modernized spelling and punctuation and inserted headings.

[4] Ibid., page 393.

[5] For a thoughtful treatment of Cranmer's eucharistic theology, see Crockett, *Eucharist: Symbol of Transformation*, pages 164-173.

[6] Ibid., page 170.

[7] 1662 Book of Common Prayer, page 345.

[8] William Nicholson, *An Exposition of the Catechism of the Church of England* (1655), Parker edition, page 179.

[9] John Cosin, *Tracts for the Times* (London: Rivington, 1840), vol. 1, tract 28, page 14.

[10] John Bramhall, A *Replication to the Bishop of Chalcedon's Survey of the Church of England's Vindication from Criminous Schism*, chapter 9, section 6, in *Works* (Library of Anglo Catholic Theology), vol. 2, page 276.

[11] *Clerus Domini*, Section V (2), in Reginald Heber, ed., *The Whole Works of the Right Reverend Jeremy Taylor, D.D., with a Life of the Author* (London, 1828), vol 14, pages 452-453. For an excellent study of Jeremy Taylor on the eucharist, see A. R. McAdoo, *The Eucharistic Theology of Jeremy Taylor* (Norwich, U.K.: Canterbury Press, 1988).

[12] John Johnson, *The Unbloody Sacrifice and Altar* (London, Part I, 1714; Part II, 1718), Part I, II:I, page 146, cited in Grisbrooke, *Anglican Liturgies of the Seventeenth and Eighteenth Centuries*, page 76.

[13] Ibid., page 238.

[14] Ibid., Part II, Introduction, pages 12-13.

[15] Ibid., Part I, I:II, pages 214-215.

[16] Grisbrooke, *Anglican Liturgies of the Seventeenth and Eighteenth Centuries*, page 177.

[17] Ibid., pages 341-346.

CHAPTER EIGHT

THE REVISED EUCHARISTIC PRAYERS OF THE TWENTIETH CENTURY

❖ ❖ ❖ ❖ ❖ ❖ ❖ ❖ ❖ ❖ ❖ ❖ ❖

THE FIRST STAGE OF REVISION: WORKING WITHIN THE TRADITIONS

The twentieth century has seen two waves of revision growing out of the Liturgical Movement in the Churches. In the first half of the century churches were engaged in revisions which moved largely within the context of their own liturgical traditions. In the Roman Catholic Church this involved recovering a style of celebration which had flourished at the formative stage of the tradition, but it did not involve actual revision of liturgical texts for the celebration of the eucharist. In the churches of the Reformation, the pattern of revision was more varied. Lutheran churches recovered something of the richness of the early Lutheran liturgies which had often been lost in intervening centuries. The liturgical pattern of Luther's Latin rite of 1523, which included the sursum corda, preface, and Sanctus gained favor over the more radical pattern of the German rite of 1526. Lutherans, however, worked with Luther's teaching that it is the proclamation of the words of Christ that consecrate the bread and wine, so that Lutheran churches did not develop full eucharistic prayers. Churches in the Reformed tradition moved in general toward a recovery of very early Reformed liturgies which retained more of the traditional shape of the eucharist. The Reformed tradition, unlike the Lutheran tradition, considered the institution narrative as a warrant, not a form of consecration, and so allowed scope for a eucharistic prayer as a prayer of consecration, even though the later liturgies of the Reformation era had generally abandoned the traditional structure for such prayers. In the early twentieth century a general movement toward a more liturgical form of worship in the Reformed tradition led to the recovery of a more classic structure for eucharistic prayers, though such prayers generally did not incorporate the institution narrative. The situation was more complex within the Anglican tradition. Revision in many parts of the Anglican Communion moved toward recovery of a full eucharistic prayer with a structure like that of the 1764 Scottish Communion Office. The Church of England itself, however, was unable to gain parliamentary consent for the revision which it undertook in the 1920s. English bishops nevertheless authorized use of the book alongside the standard rite of 1662, and parishes often adapted the authorized rites in their own way.

THE SECOND STAGE OF REVISION: MOVING TOWARD ECUMENICAL CONSENSUS

The widespread liturgical revision which took place in the second half of the century was the result of a convergence of many factors. Biblical scholarship, pursued increasingly in an ecumenical context, contributed to a clearer grasp of the roots of the Christian eucharist in Scripture and in Jewish worship. Historical liturgical scholarship offered a much clearer picture of the way in which the eucharistic liturgy and the eucharistic prayer had developed. Theological scholarship enriched our understanding of sacramental and liturgical theology and led to increasing convergence on how to address the issues of the presence of Christ in the eucharist and the eucharistic sacrifice. The ecumenical movement established a context where churches could work out the consequences of the biblical studies, liturgical studies, and theological studies in dialogue with each other. The pastoral needs of the times made the task of liturgical revision all the more urgent.

By the middle of the century liturgical scholarship had recovered a relatively clear picture of the structure of the Sunday eucharist which had developed in the second century. This is the "shape of the liturgy" which Gregory Dix made famous in his book in 1945. It is the shape to which Justin Martyr bears witness in his *First Apology*. Justin Martyr, however, gave only the outline of the rite, and it is impossible to discern just what shape the eucharistic prayer in his rite took. Liturgical scholarship in this period also uncovered what appears to be the earliest eucharistic prayer extant in the church order known as the *Apostolic Tradition* and generally attributed to Hippolytus—a work which was reconstructed from later orders which incorporated it into their texts.

This prayer appears to date back to the early third century and is the earliest known example of what we have come to call the West Syrian structure, although it lacks the Sanctus. It proved enormously influential as a model of the eucharistic prayer, and (when expanded with the Sanctus) provided for those who undertook the work of liturgical revision what generally became the standard structure for such prayers. The trinitarian shape of the classic West Syrian structure proved almost irresistibly attractive as churches began the work of crafting new eucharistic prayers. Another popular feature of new eucharistic prayers was the use of acclamations. The Byzantine anaphoras have such an acclamation between the anamnesis and the epiclesis, thus marking the transition between two sections of the eucharistic prayer. The acclamation most frequently adopted, however, was the memorial acclamation of the anaphora of St. James (or a variant of this text), which comes between the institution narrative and the anamnesis.

The impact of the West Syrian structure can be seen in the discussion of the meaning of the eucharist in the report *Baptism, Eucharist, and Ministry* adopted by the World Council of Churches in 1982.[1] The first three sections of this discussion are devoted to the Eucharist as (A) "Thanksgiving to the Father," (B) "Anamnesis or Memorial of Christ," and (C) "Invocation of the Spirit." The three sections correlate closely to (A) the preface and Sanctus, (B) the post-Sanctus, institution narrative, and anamnesis, and (C) epiclesis and supplication of West Syrian anaphoras.

A key to this discussion of the meaning of the eucharist is the rediscovery of the chief prayer of the rite as a thanksgiving (eucharistia), an exploration of the biblical meaning of anamnesis, and a new emphasis (for many) on the role of the Holy Spirit at the eucharist. The text defines anamnesis in this context as "the memorial of the crucified and risen Christ, i.e., the living and effective sign of his sacrifice, accomplished once for all on the cross and still operative on behalf of all humankind," and notes that "the biblical idea of memorial as applied to the eucharist refers to this present efficacy of God's work when it is celebrated by his people in a liturgy."[2] This definition effectively spans much of the gap between the contemporary understanding of the eucharistic sacrifice and Reformation rejection of such a doctrine.

Even the Roman canon came to be interpreted according to this structure. In this case the structure is clearly superimposed on the rite, however, rather than integral to it. The Roman canon has no invocation of the Holy Spirit and it divides its anaphoral commemorations or intercessions, with some coming after the Sanctus and some coming at the end of the prayer. The canon can only be fit into this structure if one treats two of the petitions for the acceptance of the sacrifice (Quam oblationen and Supra quae/Supplices) as the equivalents of invocations of the Spirit (first upon the gifts and then upon the communicants). The double epiclesis of the Alexandrian tradition is claimed as a precedent here, but in that tradition the epiclesis after the anamnesis, borrowed from the liturgy of St. James, is clearly consecratory in character. A model for interpreting the Roman canon in this way is the eucharistic prayer of the Reformed community of Taizé for Sundays and festivals published in 1959, which was based on the Roman canon.[3] In that prayer the anaphoral intercessions are removed, the first epiclesis is closely modelled on the Alexandrian tradition (with the link word "fill") and followed by a paraphrase of the Quam oblationem, and the paraphrase of the Supra quae/Supplices is labeled as an invocation but it does not explicitly invoke the Spirit upon the communicants. The weekday alternative follows the same model, but has an explicit invocation of the Spirit in both places.

ISSUES IN NEW EUCHARISTIC PRAYERS WITH A MODIFIED WEST SYRIAN STRUCTURE

The new eucharistic prayers of the Roman Catholic Church follow the model of Taizé, but do include anaphoral intercessions and commemorations, placing them in the Antiochene position at the end of the prayer. This modified structure also came to be adopted by other churches that understood the words of Christ as consecratory. It was adopted by the Church of England in the *Alternative Service Book*. It is the pattern of the eucharistic prayer of the Lima liturgy of the World Council of Churches. And it has been adopted in many cases by Lutheran churches, though some did use the standard West Syrian structure. Other Lutherans, insisting on Luther's doctrine of consecration by the words of Christ proclaimed as gospel, continue to reject a eucharistic prayer or even refuse to provide non-consecratory substitutes for such a prayer distinct from the institution narrative.

When the consecratory epiclesis is placed before the words of institution, however, the significance of the oblation made by many of the classical Antiochene anaphoras is altered. In the Antiochene structure, the gifts are offered, consecrated, and received. The church's offering is transformed by its identification with Christ's sacrifice and when received by communicants seals to them the benefits of Christ's sacrifice. The church's offering of bread and wine may even be described as the "antitypes" of Christ's body and blood, but the explicit identification of the gifts with his body and blood is only made through the epiclesis. The original logic of the Roman canon appears to be the same. The church's offering is described as the "figure" or the "image and likeness" of Christ's body and blood in the early forms of the Quam oblationem, but the identification is only made after the offering is accepted at the heavenly altar in the Supra quae/Supplices, and the gifts are described as the bread and the cup, not the body and blood, in the oblation during the anamnesis. The oblation even in the final form of the Roman canon, where the Quam oblationem is a petition for consecration, is ambiguous.

But when the words of Christ are understood as consecratory, what is offered in the anamnesis, though described as the bread and the cup, is the body and blood of Christ. The ambiguity in the final form of the Roman canon is resolved in Eucharistic Prayer IV of the Roman Catholic Church, where the gifts offered in the anamnesis are explicitly identified as Christ's body and blood—to the acute discomfort of many Roman Catholic liturgical scholars. That is not the understanding of the eucharistic sacrifice implicit in either the classical West Syrian prayers or the Scottish-American strand of the Anglican tradition, and it is in fact the concept that caused Reformers to reject the doctrine of eucharistic sacrifice.

Reformation churches which hold to the consecration by the words of Christ therefore are confronted with a twofold problem if they adopt the West Syrian structure. First of all, a consecratory epiclesis in the West Syrian position does not make sense. An epiclesis in this position must be an epiclesis upon the communicants, since the words of Christ are understood to be consecratiory. Any epiclesis upon the gifts must come before the institution narrative. The Church of England, therefore, has adopted the same double epiclesis as the Roman Catholic Church, and some Lutheran Churches have done the same.

The second problem is that an oblation of the gifts in the anamnesis will of necessity be an oblation of the body and blood of Christ if the words of Christ are understood to consecrate. Reformation churches have dealt with this in a variety of ways. Cranmer's 1549 eucharistic prayers actually incorporated several of them:

1. The anamnesis may be worded as a celebration and memorial of Christ's sacrifice (with or without reference to the gifts).
2. The sacrifice offered may be described as a sacrifice of praise and thanksgiving.
3. The oblation made may be the self-oblation of the communicants.

Another alternative is suggested by the West Syrian anaphora of the apostles:

4. The anamnesis may be coupled with thanksgiving rather than with oblation.

NEW EUCHARISTIC PRAYERS

The West Syrian structure presents no problems for the Scottish-American strand of the Anglican tradition, which formulated its classic prayers in this way. Other churches have dealt with the problem of the epiclesis and the oblation in various ways. Let us look at a sample prayer from the new Roman prayers and from each of the Reformation traditions which we have examined.

The Scottish-American Tradition: The Anglican Church of Canada

The Anglican Church of Canada published its new alternative eucharistic prayers in *The Book of Alternative Services* of 1985, drawing on the slightly earlier work of the Episcopal Church in the United States, which published a new edition of its Book of Common Prayer in 1976 (with final approval in 1979). Eucharistic Prayer 2 in that book is an adaptation of the anaphora from the *Apostolic Tradition:*

V. The Lord be with you
R. And also with you.
V. Lift up your hearts.
R. We lift them up to the Lord.
V. Let us give thanks to the Lord our God.
R. It is right to give our thanks and praise.

We give you thanks and praise, almighty God, through your beloved Son, Jesus Christ, our Saviour and Redeemer. He is your living Word, through whom you have created all things.

By the power of the Holy Spirit, he took flesh of the Virgin Mary and shared our human nature. He lived and died as one of us, to reconcile us to you, the God and Father of all.

In fulfilment of your will he stretched out his hands in suffering, to bring release to those who place their hope in you; and so he won for you a holy people.

He chose to bear our griefs and sorrows, and to give up his life on the cross, that he might shatter the chains of evil and death, and banish the darkness of sin and despair. By his resurrection he brings us into the light of your presence.

Now with all creation we raise our voices to proclaim the glory of your name.

> Holy, holy, holy Lord, God of power and might. Heaven and earth are full of your glory. Hosanna in the highest. Blessed is he who comes in the name of the Lord. Hosanna in the highest.

Holy and gracious God, accept our praise, through your Son our Savior Jesus Christ; who on the night he was handed over to suffering and death, took break and gave you thanks, saying, "Take, and eat: this is my body which is broken for you." In the same way he took the cup, saying, "This is my blood which is shed for you. When you do this, you do it in memory of me."

Remembering, therefore, his death and resurrection, we offer you this bread and this cup, giving thanks that you have made us worthy to stand in your presence and serve you.

We ask you to send your Holy Spirit upon the offering of your holy Church. Gather into one all who share in these sacred mysteries, filling them with the Holy Spirit and confirming their faith in the truth, that together we may praise you and give you glory through your Servant, Jesus Christ.

All glory and honour are yours, Father and Son, with the Holy Spirit in the holy Church, now and for ever. *Amen.*[4]

This prayer, like its prototype, has a single epiclesis upon both gifts and communicants that is not specifically consecratory in nature. The Sanctus has been skillfully incorporated, using a post-Sanctus which provides a short link to the institution narrative. The rubrics specify the preparing, giving thanks, breaking the bread, and administering communion at appropriate places in the rite: none of these actions is duplicated in manual acts during the institution narrative. Eucharistic Prayer 6 in this book is an adaptation of the Alexandrian anaphora of St. Basil, with a single epiclesis upon gifts and communicants that is explicitly consecratory.

The Roman Catholic Church

Eucharistic Prayer 2 of the Roman Catholic Church is also an adaptation of the anaphora of the *Apostolic Tradition*. But it has been revised to follow the modified West Syrian structure, with two epicleses and concluding intercession.

V. The Lord be with you.
R. And also with you.
V. Lift up your hearts.
R. We lift them up to the Lord.
V. Let us give thanks to the Lord our God.
R. It is right to give him thanks and praise.

Father, it is our duty and our salvation, always and everywhere to give you thanks through your beloved Son, Jesus Christ.

He is the Word through whom you made the universe, the Saviour you sent to redeem us. By the power of the Holy Spirit he took flesh and was born of the Virgin Mary.

For our sake he opened his arms on the cross; he put an end to death and revealed the resurrection. In this he fulfilled your will and won for you a holy people.

And so we join the angels and the saints in proclaiming your glory as we sing:

Holy, holy, holy Lord, God of power and might. Heaven and earth are full of your glory. Hosanna in the highest. Blessed is he who comes in the name of the Lord. Hosanna in the highest.

Lord, you are holy indeed, the fountain of all holiness. Let your Spirit come upon these gifts to make them holy, so that they may become for us the body and blood of our Lord Jesus Christ.

Before he was given up to death, a death he freely accepted, he took bread and gave you thanks. He broke the bread, gave it to his disciples, and said: Take this, all of you, and eat it: This is my body which will be given for you. When supper was ended, he took the cup. Again he gave you thanks and praise, gave the cup to his disciples, and said: Take this, all of you, and drink from it: this is the cup of my blood, the blood of the new and everlasting covenant. It will be shed for you and for all, so that sins may be forgiven. Do this in memory of me.

Let us proclaim the mystery of faith:

Christ has died, Christ is risen. Christ will come again. *Three other acclamations may be used in place of this.*

In memory of his death and resurrection, we offer you, Father, this life-giving bread, this saving cup. We thank you for counting us worthy to stand in your presence and serve you.

> May all of us who share in the body and blood of Christ be brought together in unity by the Holy Spirit.
>
> Lord, remember your Church throughout the world; make us grow in love as your people, together with N. our Pope, N. our bishop, and all the ministers of your Gospel.
>
> Remember our brothers and sisters who have gone to their rest in the hope of rising again; bring them and all the departed into the light of your presence.
>
> Have mercy upon all; make us worthy to share eternal life with Mary, the virgin mother of God, with the apostles, and with all the saints who have done your will throughout the ages. May we praise you in union with them, and give you glory through your Son, Jesus Christ.
>
> Through him, and with him, and in him, in the unity of the Holy Spirit, all glory and honour is yours, almighty Father, for ever and ever. *Amen.*[5]

Notice how the model has been modified here. The Sanctus has been added, as in the Anglican adaptation above. But here the epiclesis has also been divided, with an epiclesis over the gifts before the institution narrative, and an epiclesis over the communicants in the original place. The oblation in the anamnesis has the same ambiguity as that in the Roman canon: the gifts are described as bread and wine, but according to the theology of the modified West Syrian model, the consecration has already occurred. The traditional manual acts are prescribed during the institution narrative. A memorial acclamation has been added. Notice also that intercessions and commemorations have been added at the end of the prayer. Eucharistic Prayer IV is an adaptation of the Alexandrian anaphora of Basil. The same modifications have been made here. But in this case the gifts in the oblation are actually described as the body and blood of Christ.

The Church of England:
The English Strand of the Anglican Tradition

Apparently out of commitment to a theology of consecration by the words of Christ, the Church of England adopted the double epiclesis which we find in Roman Catholic prayers. That required a modification of the anamnesis, however, for a church in the Reformation tradition. The Second Eucharistic Prayer of the *Alternative Service Book* shows how the West Syrian structure was modified in this tradition.

V. The Lord be with you.   *or*   V. The Lord is here.

R. And also with you.   *R.* His Spirit is with us.

V. Lift up your hearts.

R. We lift them up to the Lord.

V. Let us give thanks to the Lord our God.

R. It is right to give him thanks and praise.

It is indeed right, it is our duty and our joy, at all times and in all places to give you thanks and praise, holy Father, heavenly King, almighty and eternal God, through Jesus Christ your only Son our Lord.

For he is your living Word; through him you have created all things from the beginning, and formed us in your own image.

Through him you have freed us from the slavery of sin, giving him to be born as a man and to die upon the cross; you raised him from the dead and exalted him to your right hand on high.

Through him you have sent upon us your holy and life-giving Spirit, and made us a people for your own possession.

A proper preface may follow.

Therefore with angels and archangels, and with all the company of heaven, we proclaim your great and glorious name, for ever praising you and saying:

> Holy, holy, holy Lord, God of power and might. Heaven and earth are full of your glory. Hosanna in the highest. Blessed is he who comes in the name of the Lord. Hosanna in the highest.

Hear us, heavenly Father, through Jesus Christ your Son our Lord, through him accept our sacrifice of praise; and grant that by the power of your Holy Spirit these gifts of bread and wine may be to us his body and his blood;

Who on the same night that he was betrayed, took bread and gave you thanks; he broke it and gave it to his disciples, saying, Take, eat; this is my body which is given for you; do this in remembrance of me. In the same way, after supper he took the cup and gave you thanks; he gave it to them, saying, Drink this, all of you; this is my blood of the new covenant, which is shed for you and for many for the forgiveness of sins. Do this, as often as you drink it, in remembrance of me.

> Christ has died; Christ is risen: Christ will come again.

Therefore, Lord and heavenly Father, having in remembrance his death once for all upon the cross, his resurrection from the dead, and his ascension into heaven, and looking for the coming of his kingdom, we make with this bread and this cup the memorial of Christ your Son our Lord.

Accept through him this offering of our duty and service, and as we eat and drink these holy gifts in the presence of your divine majesty, fill us with your grace and heavenly blessing; nourish us with the body and blood of your Son, that we may grow into his likeness, and, made one by your Spirit, become a living temple to your glory.

Through Jesus Christ our Lord, by whom, and with whom, and in whom, in the unity of the Holy Spirit, all honour and glory be yours, almighty Father, from all who stand before you in earth and heaven, now and for ever. *Amen.*[6]

Here too we find a double epiclesis, although the invocation of the Spirit upon the communicants is quite indirect. What is noteworthy here, however, is the awkward handling of the oblation and the second epiclesis. The anamnesis itself is a variant of the 1549 form; the following paragraph is a very weak form of an epiclesis on the communicants. It is unclear what is gained here by the phrase "as we eat and drink these holy gifts in the presence of your divine majesty." No manual acts are prescribed.

The Lutheran Tradition:
The Evangelical Lutheran Church in America

We have already noted two problems that the standard West Syrian structure raises for Lutherans: the words of Christ (which Luther understood as consecratory) come before the epiclesis in the West Syrian structure and an oblation in the anamnesis comes after the words of Christ in this structure. However the structure is adapted, the wording of the anamnesis will require attention. Some Lutheran churches have followed the modified West Syrian structure with a double epiclesis. The Evangelical Lutheran Church in America has opted for a single epiclesis which invokes the Spirit after the anamnesis. For the sake of Lutheran sensibilities, however, it has had to provide also for the proclamation of the institution narrative without the continuation of the eucharistic prayer after the Sanctus or for such a proclamation after an adapted conclusion to the prayer.

V. The Lord be with you.
R. And also with you.
V. Lift up your hearts.
R. We lift them up to the Lord.
V. Let us give thanks to the Lord our God.
R. It is right to give him thanks and praise.

It is right and salutary that we should at all times and in all places offer thanks and praise to you, O Lord, holy Father, through Jesus Christ our Lord. And so, with the Church on earth and the hosts of heaven, we praise your name and join their unending hymn.

A proper preface may replace this preface, which is the ordinary weekday preface.

Holy, holy, holy Lord, God of power and might. Heaven and earth are full of your glory. Hosanna in the highest. Blessed is he who comes in the name of the Lord. Hosanna in the highest.

Full Eucharistic Prayer	**"Prayer of Thanksgiving" with Words of Christ**	**Words of Christ Alone**
Holy God, mighty Lord, gracious Father: Endless is your mercy and eternal your reign. You have filled all creation with light and life. Through Abraham you promised to bless all nations. You rescued Israel, your chosen people. Through the prophets you renewed your promise; and, at this end of all the ages, you sent your son, who in words and deeds proclaimed your kingdom and was obedient to your will, even to giving his life.	Blessed are you, Lord of heaven and earth. In mercy for our fallen world you gave your only Son, that all those who believe in him should not perish, but have eternal life. We give thanks to you for the salvation you have prepared for us through Jesus Christ. Send now your Holy Spirit into our hearts, that we may receive our Lord with a living faith as he comes to us in his holy supper. Amen. Come, Lord Jesus.	
In the night in which he was betrayed, our Lord Jesus Christ took bread, and gave thanks; broke it, and gave it to his disciples, saying: Take and eat; this is my body, given for you. Do this for the remembrance of me. Again, after supper, he took the cup, gave thanks, and gave it for all to drink, saying: This cup is the new covenant in my blood, shed for you and for all people for the forgiveness of sins. Do this for the remembrance of me.	In the night in which he was betrayed, our Lord Jesus Christ took bread, and gave thanks; broke it, and gave it to his disciples, saying: Take and eat; this is my body, given for you. Do this for the remembrance of me. Again, after supper, he took the cup, gave thanks, and gave it for all to drink, saying: This cup is the new covenant in my blood, shed for you and for all people for the forgiveness of sins. Do this for the remembrance of me.	In the night in which he was betrayed, our Lord Jesus Christ took bread, and gave thanks; broke it, and gave it to his disciples, saying: Take and eat; this is my body, given for you. Do this for the remembrance of me. Again, after supper, he took the cup, gave thanks, and gave it for all to drink, saying: This cup is the new covenant in my blood, shed for you and for all people for the forgiveness of sins. Do this for the remembrance of me.
For as often as we eat of this bread and drink of this cup, we proclaim the Lord's death until he comes. Christ has died. Christ is risen. Christ will come again.		

The Full Eucharistic Prayer continues at this point. *The other two options conclude.*

Therefore, gracious Father, with this bread and cup we remember the life our Lord offered for us. And believing the witness of his resurrection, we await his coming in power to share with us the great and promised feast.

Amen. Come, Lord Jesus.

Send now, we pray, your Holy Spirit, the spirit of our Lord and of his resurrection, that we who receive the Lord's body and blood may live to the praise of your glory and receive our inheritance with all your saints in light.

Amen. Come, Holy Spirit.

Join our prayers with those of your servants in every time and place and unite them with the ceaseless petitions of our great high priest until he comes as victorious Lord of all. Through him, with him, in him, in the unity of the Holy Spirit, all honor and glory is yours, almighty Father, now and for ever. *Amen.*[7]

Eucharistic Prayer II has the same responses as Prayer I, and the post-Sanctus, anamnesis, and epiclesis of the two prayers are interchangeable. Eucharistic Prayer III has the same components as the first two, but uses no acclamations between the sections of the prayer. Eucharistic Prayer IV is a relatively close translation of the anaphora of the *Apostolic Tradition* and omits the Sanctus. Note the epiclesis in Prayer I (which is paralleled in Prayer II): it invokes the Holy Spirit without specifying upon what or whom it is invoked. Prayer III, surprisingly, invokes the Word and Spirit upon both the communicants and the gifts, but its result clause asks a blessing for the communicants. Prayer IV, true to the original text, invokes the Spirit upon the gifts but is not consecratory. The anamnesis in Prayers I and II is a remembrance only, without either an oblation or a thanksgiving, but it is made with the bread and the cup. Prayer III asks God to accept the church's praise and thanksgiving. Prayer IV alters the verb of the anamnesis from "offer" to "lift." The use of the three acclamations to punctuate the divisions of the prayer is interesting.

It is clear that the drafters wished to move away from Luther's doctrine of consecration by the words of Christ alone to a more nuanced approach. Even though they were compelled to offer two alternative approaches to a full eucharistic prayer, it is remarkable that they were able to offer full eucharistic prayers with the classic West Syrian structure.

The Reformed Tradition: The Church of Scotland

The Church of Scotland's *Book of Common Order* of 1979 is a good representative of the Reformed tradition, although its approach to language is more traditional than that adopted by most other churches at the time. The warrant may be read separately, before the eucharistic prayer, following older Reformed usage, or incorporated into the prayer. The institution narrative is repeated, as in the Westminister Directory, after the Prayer, as the minister performs the manual acts. The order given below is the second of three, and uses the language conventions of the Revised Standard Version of the Bible.

Prayer of the Veil and Offertory Prayer

when the minister shall unveil the elements.

Let us pray:

O God, who by the blood of thy dear Son hast consecrated for us a new and living way into the holiest of all; help us in faith to enter with him and grant that being pure in heart by grace, we may have part in his true, pure, immortal sacrifice; through Jesus Christ our Lord. Amen.

Almighty and most merciful Father, out of the fullness of thy gifts, we offer to thee this bread and this cup. Blessed be thy holy name for ever; through Jesus Christ our Lord. Amen.

If the words of institution included in the prayer of consecration below are not to be used, the warrant may be read here.

[Beloved in the Lord, attend to the words of the institution of the holy supper of our Lord Jesus Christ, as they are delivered by Saint Paul.

I have received of the Lord that which also I delivered unto you, that the Lord Jesus, the same night in which he was betrayed, took bread; and when he had given thanks, he brake it, and said, Take, eat: this is my body which is broken for you; this do in remembrance of me. After the same manner also he took the cup, when he had supped, saying, This cup is the new testament in my blood; this do ye, as oft as ye drink it, in remembrance of me. For as often as ye eat this bread, and drink this cup, ye do shew the Lord's death till he come.]

The Eucharistic Prayer

V. The Lord be with you.

R. And with thy spirit.

V. Lift up your hearts.

R. We lift them up unto the Lord.

V. Let us give thanks unto our Lord God.

R. It is meet and right so to do.

Truly at all times and in all places we should give thanks to thee, O holy Lord, Father Almighty, everlasting God: who didst create the heavens and the earth and all that is therein; who didst make man in thine own image and whose tender mercies are over all thy works.

We praise thee for Jesus Christ whom thou hast sent to be the Savior of the world. Blessed be the hour in which he was born and the hour in which he died. Blessed be the dawn of his rising again and the high day of his ascending.

We praise thee that he, having ascended up on high and sitting at thy right hand, sent forth thy Holy Spirit upon the Church to be the light and guide of all those who put their trust in thee. Blessed be the Spirit, the Giver of Life, enabling thy people to proclaim the gospel among all nations and to fulfill with Christ their royal priesthood until he comes again.

Thee, mighty God, heavenly King, we magnify and praise. With angels and archangels and with all the company of heaven, we worship and adore thy glorious name, evermore praising thee and saying:

> Holy, holy, holy, Lord God of hosts. Heaven and earth are full of thy glory. Glory be to thee, O Lord Most High. Blessed is he that cometh in the name of the Lord. Hosanna in the highest.

Truly holy and blessed is thy Son Jesus Christ, blessed in all his gifts, blessed in that most holy mystery which he did institute, who in the same night in which he was betrayed, took bread; and when he had blessed and given thanks he broke it and said, "Take, eat: this is my body which is broken for you; do this in remembrance of me." In the same manner also after supper he took the cup, saying, "This cup is the new covenant in my blood; do this, as often as you shall drink it, in remembrance of me."

Therefore, having in remembrance his work and passion, we now plead his eternal sacrifice and set forth this memorial which he has commanded us to make. Send down thy Holy Spirit to sanctify both us and these thine own gifts of bread and wine which we set before thee, that the bread which we break may be the communion of the body of Christ, and the cup which we bless the communion of the blood of Christ; that we may receive them to our spiritual nourishment and growth in grace, and to the glory of thy most holy name.

These things, O Lord, we seek not only for ourselves but for all in the communion of thy Church and especially for...*[here the minister may pray for the sick, and the poor, and for the needs of particular persons; or a short period of silence may be kept.]*

Accept this our duty and service, O Father, and graciously accept us also as, in fellowship with all the faithful in heaven and on earth, we pray thee to fulfill in us, and in all men, the purpose of thy redeeming love; through Jesus Christ our Lord, in whose words we are bold to pray and to say,

Our Father....

The Breaking of the Bread

[V. Holy things to the holy:
R. One only is holy, Jesus Christ, in whom we are to the glory of God the Father.
V. O taste and see that the Lord is good:
R. Blessed is the man that trusteth in him.]

Here the minister shall say: In obedience to our Lord Jesus Christ, and for a memorial of him we do this: who, the same night in which he was betrayed, took bread (*here the minister shall take the bread into his hands*), and when he had blessed, and given thanks, he broke it (*here he shall break the bread*), and said, "Take, eat: this is my body which is broken for you: do this in remembrance of me." After the same manner also, he took the cup (*here he shall raise the cup*), saying, "This cup is the new covenant in my blood: do this, as often as you shall drink it, in remembrance of me."

Lamb of God, that takest away the sins of the world: Have mercy upon us.
Lamb of God, that takest away the sins of the world: Have mercy upon us.
Lamb of God, that takest away the sins of the world: Grant us thy peace.[8]

This is a confident adaptation of the traditional West Syrian structure by a church that has a long tradition of a prayer of consecration. The Calvinist tradition of pleading the sacrifice of Christ rather than offering that sacrifice finds articulate expression in the anamnesis.[9] The prayer has been carefully crafted, so that it flows well even if the institution narrative is omitted and read first as a warrant.

The Reformed Tradition: The Presbyterian Church (U.S.A.)

In the United States, the Presbyterian Church is perhaps the foremost representative of the Reformed tradition. Its *Book of Common Worship* offers a selection of eucharistic prayers which also follow the West Syrian structure (although they also provide for the use of the institution account before the Great Thanksgiving as an invitation [warrant] and after the Great Thanksgiving during the breaking of bread—the traditional places for this account in the Reformed tradition). The carefully organized structure of these prayers and their eloquent contemporary language make them among the finest of the contemporary eucharistic prayers in the English language. The excerpt which follows is from the Service for the Lord's Day in the *Book of Common Worship*.

INVITATION TO THE LORD'S TABLE

Standing at the table, the presiding minister invites the people to the Sacrament, using one of the following or another invitation to the Lord's Table. If B is used, the words of institution are not included in the great thanksgiving or at the breaking of the bread.

A   *See Luke 13:29 and Luke 24:30, 31*

Friends, this is the joyful feast of the people of God! They will come from east and west, and from north and south, and sit at table in the kingdom of God.

According to Luke, when our Lord was at table with his disciples, he took the bread, and blessed and broke it, and gave it to them. Their eyes were opened and they recognized him.

This is the Lord's table. Our Savior invites those who trust him to share the feast which he has prepared.

B   *See 1 Cor. 11:23-26; Luke 22:11-19*

Hear the words of the institution of the Holy Supper of our Lord Jesus Christ:

The Lord Jesus, on the night of his arrest, took bread, and after giving thanks to God, he broke it, and gave it to his disciples, saying: Take, eat. This is my body, given for you. Do this in remembrance of me.

In the same way he took the cup, saying: This cup is the new covenant in my blood, shed for you for the forgiveness of sins. Whenever you drink it, do this in remembrance of me.

Every time you eat this bread and drink this cup, you proclaim the saving death of the risen Lord, until he comes.

With thanksgiving, let us offer God our grateful praise.

GREAT THANKSGIVING

The people stand.

The presiding minister leads the people in the following or another great thanksgiving appropriate to the season or occasion:

Great Thanksgiving A

V. The Lord be with you.

R. And also with you.

V. Lift up your hearts.

R. We lift them to the Lord.

V. Let us give thanks to the Lord our God.

R. It is right to give our thanks and praise.

It is truly right and our greatest joy to give you thanks and praise, O Lord our God, creator and ruler of the universe. In your wisdom you made all things and sustain them by your power. You formed us in your image, setting us in this world to love and serve you, and to live at peace with your whole creation. When we rebelled against you, refusing to trust and obey you, you did not reject us, but still claimed us as your own. You sent prophets to call us back to your way.

Then in the fullness of time, out of your great love for the world, you sent your only Son to be one of us, to redeem us and heal our brokenness.

Therefore we praise you, joining our voices with choirs of angels, with prophets, apostles, and martyrs, and with all the faithful of every time and place, who forever sing to the glory of your name:

The people may sing or say:

Holy, holy, holy Lord, God of power and might.
Heaven and earth are full of your glory.
Hosanna in the highest.
Blessed is he who comes in the name of the Lord.
Hosanna in the highest.

The minister continues:

You are holy, O God of majesty, and blessed is Jesus Christ, your Son, our Lord. In Jesus, born of Mary, your Word became flesh and dwelt among us, full of grace and truth. He lived as one of us, knowing sorrow and joy. He healed the sick, fed the hungry, opened blind eyes, broke bread with outcasts and sinners, and proclaimed the good news of your kingdom to the poor and needy. Dying on the cross, he gave himself for the life of the world. Rising from the grave, he won for us victory over death. Seated at your right hand, he leads us to eternal life. We praise you that Christ now reigns with you in glory, and will come again to make all things new.

If they have not already been said, the words of institution may be said here, or in relation to the breaking of the bread.

We give thanks that the Lord Jesus, on the night before he died, took bread, and after giving thanks to you, he broke it, and gave it to his disciples, saying: Take, eat. This is my body, given for you. Do this in remembrance of me.

In the same way he took the cup, saying: This cup is the new covenant sealed in my blood, shed for you for the forgiveness of sins. Whenever you drink it, do this in remembrance of me.

Remembering your gracious acts in Jesus Christ, we take from your creation this bread and this wine and joyfully celebrate his dying and rising, as we await the day of his coming. With thanksgiving, we offer our very selves to you, to be a living and holy sacrifice, dedicated to your service.

The people may sing or say one of the following [the first line of each is the introductory cue by the minister]:

1   Great is the mystery of faith:
     Christ has died, Christ is risen, Christ will come again.

2   Praise to you, Lord Jesus:
     Dying you destroyed our death, rising you restored our life.
     Lord Jesus, come in glory.

3   According to his commandment:
     We remember his death, we proclaim his resurrection, we
     await his coming in glory.

4   Christ is the bread of life:
     When we eat this bread and drink this cup, we proclaim
     your death, Lord Jesus, until you come in glory.

     The minister continues:

Gracious God, pour out your Holy Spirit upon us and upon these your gifts of bread and wine, that the bread we break and the cup we bless may be the communion of the body and blood of Christ. By your Spirit make us one with Christ, that we may be one with all who share this feast, united in every place. As this bread is Christ's body for us, send us out to be the body of Christ in the world.

Intercessions for the church and the world may be included here, using these or similar prayers.

Remember your church.... Unite it in the truth of your Word and empower it in ministry to the world.

Remember the world of nations.... By your Spirit renew the face of the earth; let peace and justice prevail.

Remember our family and friends.... Bless them and watch over them; be gracious to them and give them peace.

Remember the sick and the suffering, the aged and the dying.... Encourage them and give them hope.

Rejoicing in the communion of saints, we remember with thanksgiving all your faithful servants, and those dear to us, whom you have called from this life....

We are grateful that for them death is no more, nor is there sorrow, crying, or pain, for the former things have passed away.

In union with your church in heaven and on earth, we pray, O God, that you will fulfill your eternal purpose in us and in all the world.

Keep us faithful in your service until Christ comes in final victory, and we shall feast with all your saints in the joy of your eternal realm.

Through Christ, with Christ, in Christ, in the unity of the Holy Spirit, all glory and honor are yours, almighty Father, now and for ever. *Amen.*

LORD'S PRAYER

BREAKING OF THE BREAD

> *If the words of institution have not previously been said, the minister breaks the bread, using A.*

> *If the words of institution were said in the invitation to the Lord's table or were included in the great thanksgiving, the minister breaks the bread, using B. Or the bread may be broken in silence.*

A   *See 1 Cor. 11:23-26; Luke 22:19-20*

The minister breaks the bread in full view of the people, saying:

The Lord Jesus, on the night of his arrest, took bread, and after giving thanks to God, he broke it, and gave it to his disciples, saying: Take, eat. This is my body, given for you. Do this in remembrance of me.

The minister lifts the cup saying:

In the same way he took the cup, saying: This cup is the new covenant in my blood, shed for you for the forgiveness of sins. Whenever you drink it, do this in remembrance of me.

Every time you eat this bread and drink this cup, you proclaim the saving death of the risen Lord, until he comes.

B   *1 Cor. 10:16-17*

Because there is one loaf, we, many as we are, are one body; for it is one loaf of which we partake.

The minister takes the loaf and breaks it in full view of the people, saying:

When we break the bread, is it not a sharing in the body of Christ?

Having filled the cup, the minister lifts it in the view of the people, saying:

When we give thanks over the cup, is it not a sharing in the blood of Christ?[10]

Besides Great Thanksgiving A, the *Book of Common Worship* includes a wide range of eucharistic prayers, including an unaltered translation of the eucharistic prayer of the *Apostolic Tradition* (G) and the common North American form of the anaphora of St. Basil (F). Also included are a partial text (I), with dialogue, conclusion of the preface and the Sanctus, institution narrative, anamnesis, memorial acclamations, invocation, and doxology, and a detailed outline (J) without text. Structurally all the forms follow the general West Syrian pattern. In some the institution narrative is optional (A, B, C, D, I, J); in others it is an integral part of the prayer (E, F, G); in one it is omitted (H). Prayers B, C, D, E, and I include the acclamations given in A; F has its proper acclamation, while G and H have none. Prayers B, C, and D include proper prefaces. Several of the prayers provide for proper intercessions in the supplication. The anamnesis includes an oblation of bread and wine only in prayers taken from other sources (F, G, H). American Presbyterians have not followed the Church of Scotland, which rooted its anamnesis in Hebrews and "pleaded" Christ's sacrifice and set forth the eucharist as the memorial of that sacrifice. Instead, its general preference is to word the anamnesis in terms of a sacrifice of praise and thanksgiving and the communicant's self-oblation. The epiclesis (usually upon both the gifts and the communicants) in these prayers most frequently asks that the bread and wine may be "the communion of the body and blood" of Christ. Prayer G (Hippolytus), however, has an epiclesis on the gifts alone, while Prayer H has an epiclesis upon the communicants alone. Prayers C and F ask more directly for the transformation of the gifts into the body and blood of Christ, while G (Hippolytus) focuses exclusively on the communicants in the result clause of the epiclesis. We should also note that the memorial acclamations in the various prayers come at the conclusion of the anamnesis, rather than separating the anamnesis from the institution narrative.

Elsewhere in the book proper eucharistic prayers are provided for major feasts and seasons. These prayers generally have a proper preface, post-Sanctus, and supplication, and take the remainder of their texts from Prayer A or B. The eucharistic prayer for Maundy Thursday stipulates the use of the institution narrative in the invitation (warrant), and so excludes it from the great thanksgiving and the breaking of the bread. It should be remembered that use of this rich provision of texts for the eucharistic prayer is suggested, not mandated; ministers are free also to formulate their own prayer, provided that it follows the outline prescribed in the description of the Service for the Lord's Day.

Other Major North American Churches

The United Church of Christ (in the Reformed tradition) and the United Methodist Church (whose eucharistic rite derives from the Anglican tradition) have both issued service books with eucharistic prayers which follow the West Syrian structure. The rites in the United Church of Christ's *Book of Worship* depart from the earlier Reformed tradition and incorporate the institution narrative in their prayers, but on the whole their language is less felicitous than the Presbyterian Church's rites in its *Book of Common Worship.* The first two rites in the United Methodist Church's *Hymnal* provide eucharistic prayers that are quite similar to those of the Presbyterian Church; like the Presbyterian Church, the United Methodists have also provided seasonal variants of these prayers in supplemental resources. The virtue of the way in which the United Methodist prayers are formulated is that the cue phrases which lead into the Sanctus and the acclamation are standard in all the prayers, so that it is not necessary for congregations to have the full printed text of the prayers to know when to respond. The memorial acclamation is also placed, as in the Presbyterian prayers, after the anamnesis. *The United Methodist Hymnal* also provides a rite in traditional language; here the eucharistic prayer is a slight adaptation of the Scottish rite of 1637 (which places the epiclesis before the institution narrative).

✦ ✦ ✦ ✦ ✦ ✦ ✦ ✦

The West Syrian structure has worked well for churches that have adopted it. The modified structure, however, creates a variety of problems—particularly in how the doctrine of eucharistic sacrifice will be articulated in the anamnesis, where an oblation of the elements is ordinarily made in this tradition. This appears most acute in the eucharistic prayers of the English Anglicans, where references to the bread and wine in the anamnesis and epiclesis seem infelicitous and largely gratuitous. Lutherans and the Reformed have both found it necessary to provide alternatives which separate the eucharistic prayer from the institution narrative. Ironically, the significance of the separation is reversed in the two traditions. Lutheran tradition holds that the words of Christ are consecratory; therefore the eucharistic prayer is for strict Lutherans superfluous. For the Reformed, the eucharistic prayer is consecratory, while the institution narrative functions as the warrant.

It is also interesting to note the way in which two ancient eucharistic prayers have been adapted in various traditions. The prayer from the *Apostolic Tradition* has been very popular. Two traditions which we have reviewed (the *Book of Alternative Services* of the Anglican Church of Canada and the Roman Catholic Church) have adapted it to contemporary norms by incorporating the Sanctus. The Roman Catholic adaptation, unfortunately, violates the rationale of the prayer's structure by splitting the epiclesis in two. American Lutherans have adopted the prayer without the Sanctus, slightly revising the oblation in the anamnesis by substituting the verb "lift" for the verb "offer" in the anamnesis. Adaptations of the Alexandrian anaphora of St. Basil follow a similar pattern. It has been adopted with little revision by North American churches of the Reformation, while the Roman Catholic adaptation once again splits the epiclesis and then compounds the issues this raises by making an explicit oblation of Christ's body and blood in the anamnesis.

We will look back on the contemporary scene in the conclusion to analyze how contemporary eucharistic prayers reflect the theological rationale behind the evolution of the prayer.

NOTES

[1] The text may be found in John Leith, ed., *Creeds of the Churches* (3rd ed., Louisville, Ky.: John Knox Press, 1982), pages 604-658, pages 617-631 for the section on the eucharist.

[2] "Eucharist," II.B.5, in *Creeds of the Churches*, page 620.

[3] English text in *Eucharist at Taizé* (London: Faith Press, 1962).

[4] *The Book of Alternative Services of the Anglican Church of Canada* (Toronto: Anglican Book Centre, 1985), pages 196-197.

[5] Text from Max Thurian and Geoffrey Wainwright, eds., *Baptism and Eucharist: Ecumenical Convergence in Celebration* (Grand Rapids: Eerdsmans, 1983), pages 115-117.

[6] *The Alternative Service Book 1980* (London: Holder and Stoughton, 1980), pages 133-135.

[7] *Lutheran Book of Worship: Minister's Desk Edition* (Minneapolis: Augsburg Publishing House, 1978), pages 207-225.

[8] Thurian and Wainwright, eds., *Baptism and Eucharist,* pages 156-158.

[9] On the way in which this prayer employs the theology of the letter to the Hebrews, see Bryan D. Spinks, "The Ascension and the Vicarious Humanity of Christ: The Christology and Soteriology Behind the Church of Scotland's Anamnesis and Epiklesis," in J. Neil Alexander, ed., *Time and Community* (Washington, D.C.: Pastoral Press, 1990), pages 185-201.

[10] *Book of Common Worship,* prepared by the Theology and Worship Ministry Unit for the Presbyterian Church (U.S.A.) and the Cumberland Presbyterian Church (Louisville, Ky.: Westminster/John Knox Press, 1993), pages 68-74. Other eucharistic prayers are found on pages 126-156. Seasonal variants are found in the section entitled "Resources for the Church Year," and variants are also found in the rites for Christian Marriage, the Funeral, and Ministry to the Sick.

THE EUCHARISTIC PRAYER
STRUCTURE AND COMPONENTS

✦ ✦ ✦ ✦ ✦ ✦ ✦ ✦ ✦ ✦ ✦ ✦ ✦

B y the mid-twentieth century many liturgical scholars, analyzing the texts of eucharistic prayers from the early centuries that have come down to us, believed that they could find in them a common set of components and a common pattern or structure. This structure could be described as a modest expansion of the structure of the eucharistic prayer of the *Apostolic Tradition*. W. Jardine Grisbrooke summarized this perspective in an article on the anaphora in the *New Westminster Dictionary of Liturgy and Worship*. This mid-century consensus is reflected in most of the eucharistic prayers composed in the late twentieth century. According to Grisbrooke's analysis the standard components of the eucharistic prayer are as follows:

1. introductory dialogue;
2. preface or first part of the thanksgiving;
3. Sanctus;
4. post-Sanctus or second part of the thanksgiving;
5. preliminary epiclesis (alternative or additional post-Sanctus);
6. narrative of the institution;
7. anamnesis;
8. epiclesis;

9. diptychs or intercessions, which may be divided;
10. concluding doxology.[1]

In actual fact no classical eucharistic prayer includes all these components in this sequence. It is a structure which first appeared in the eucharistic liturgy of Taizé and then in the new eucharistic prayers of the Roman Catholic Church. Grisbrooke analyzes the order of components in the classic prayers of the ancient liturgical traditions as follows:

West Syrian	1/2/3/4/6/7/8/9/10
East Syrian	1/2/3/4/6/7/9/8/10
Alexandrian	1/2a/9/2b/3/5/6/7/8/10
Roman	1/2/3/9a/5/6/7/8/9b/10
Gallican/Mozarabic	1/2/3/4/6/(7)/8/10[2]

Three comments are in order about Grisbrooke's description of the components. First, as we have seen in earlier chapters, a distinction should be made between the preface (or initial thanksgiving) and the pre-Sanctus, the introduction that links the Sanctus to the thanksgiving of the preface. Second, anaphoral intercessions and diptychs are not the same thing and should not be confused with each other.[3] Third, the sections of the Roman canon described as epicleses are in origin petitions for the acceptance of the church's offering and are not really directly comparable to the epiclesis in the Eastern traditions. Apart from this, the sequence of components listed by Grisbrooke for the various traditions is roughly accurate, but it disguises very real differences between the thematic structure of the eucharistic prayer in the various traditions, and it overlooks the fact that different traditions arrived at this sequence by very different paths.

THE ORIGINAL NUCLEUS OF THE EUCHARISTIC PRAYER

There is a growing consensus today that the nucleus from which the eucharistic prayers of the fourth century developed was a Christian form of the Jewish *Birkat ha-Mazon*. This is the basis of such common structure as we find in eucharistic prayers, not the modified West Syrian structure with which Grisbrooke is working. The nucleus was bipartite or tripartite, moving from one or two strophes of praise and thanksgiving to a strophe of supplication (for the church, sometimes formulated as a petition for the communicants). The early form of the anaphora of St. Mark found in the Strasbourg Papyrus reveals just such a nucleus, with two strophes of thanksgiving but with a supplication that has already been expanded.

The shape that the eucharistic prayer would take in the various traditions depended on how this nucleus was expanded. Except for the later version of the anaphora of St. Mark, most traditions expanded the thanksgiving with narrative elements. Eastern traditions expanded the thanksgiving into a fixed narrative of God's work in creation and redemption; Western traditions developed a variable thanksgiving in the preface, celebrating individual works of redemption which were coordinated with the feast or the season in proper prefaces. Except for the Gallican and Mozarabic traditions, later eucharistic prayers generally expanded the supplication as well with anaphoral intercessions which often included the same scope of concerns which we find in the prayers of the people in the liturgy of the word. The original supplication for the church was also expanded into an epiclesis in the east and a petition for the fruits of communion in the West.

ADDITIONAL BLOCKS OF MATERIAL

This material was expanded by two later blocks of material. The first of these blocks included the Sanctus and its introduction. In the Alexandrian tradition (and perhaps that of Jerusalem as well) an epiclesis upon the church's offering was linked to the Sanctus. This material was incorporated in different ways in different traditions. In the West Syrian tradition it was used to conclude the first thanksgiving. In the Roman tradition it was used to conclude the whole thanksgiving and was followed by the supplication. In the Alexandrian tradition it was simply appended to the old nucleus. Its original function was to give expression to the sacramental union between the eucharistic worship of the church and the worship offered at the heavenly altar. It appears to be an integral part of the eucharistic prayer described by Cyril of Jerusalem. It has the same function in the Alexandrian tradition, but has been appended to the older nucleus, coming after the supplication. In other West Syrian anaphoras this function recedes and the Sanctus becomes more an embellishment to the eucharistic prayer and less an integral part of it. In the Roman tradition it is even less an integral part of the prayer and appears to be the latest major component added to the Roman canon.

The other block of material added to the original nucleus is the institution narrative and the anamnesis which is usually linked to it. Its original function seems to have been as a citation of the warrant for the celebration of the eucharist. This material was incorporated into the anaphora in different ways in different traditions. In West Syrian anaphoras, it was included in the thanksgiving, forming the conclusion to the section of the thanksgiving which began with the post-Sanctus. In the early forms of the Roman canon, it was added not to the thanksgiving, but to the supplication, as part of a petition for the acceptance of the church's offering. In the Gallican and Mozarabic traditions, only the institution narrative was incorporated as a fixed component, though some of the variable post-pridie sections served as anamneses. In these traditions, the narrative eventually functioned more as "words of consecration" than as a warrant — as it did eventually in the Roman canon. Finally, in the anaphora of St. Mark, the institution narrative, the anamnesis, *and a consecratory epiclesis* seem to have been borrowed as a unit from the anaphora of St. James and simply appended to the end of the anaphora, which had already been expanded by the pre-Sanctus, Sanctus, and its epiclesis. As we reflect on the very different ways that this block of material was added in the different traditions, we can see that only in the West Syrian and early Roman traditions does it retain its original function; in other traditions, its function has shifted.

The Thanksgiving in Classic Eucharistic Prayers

Of the surviving eucharistic prayers, only the anaphora of St. Mark appears to have retained the brief general thanksgiving (two strophes) characteristic of the original nucleus. Characteristically, the brief summary thanksgiving of the early eucharistic prayers was replaced by a narrative thanksgiving for God's work of creation and redemption. Western traditions kept the thanksgiving to its original length by making the thanksgiving (the preface) variable and relating it to a feast or season of the celebration. In the Roman tradition the Sanctus (a late addition) concluded the thanksgiving. The West Syrian anaphoras retained a fixed thanksgiving, expanding it with the Sanctus (which concludes the first section), and the post-Sanctus, institution narrative, and anamnesis (which constitute the second section of the thanksgiving).

Structurally the thanksgiving of all the West Syrian anaphoras is the same, but thematically there was wide variation. The preface might be devoted to general praise of God (as in the anaphoras of Basil) or to a thanksgiving for creation (as in the anaphora of James) or to a brief thanksgiving for the whole work of creation and redemption (as in the anaphora of the apostles and its later derivatives). The thanksgiving of the post-Sanctus was generally Christological in character, but in the anaphora of the apostles and its derivatives it is little more than a link to the institution narrative. The anaphora of St. James is the most carefully crafted in this section: the post-Sanctus, institution narrative, and anamnesis have been carefully integrated in a single chronological sequence of thanksgiving for the work of Christ.

THE SUPPLICATION IN CLASSIC EUCHARISTIC PRAYERS

The petition for the church in the original nucleus of the eucharistic prayer was expanded in all the traditions except the Mozarabic and the Gallican into a general intercession not unlike that which we find in the prayers of the people in the liturgy of the word. The commemorations in this intercession were generally formulated in one of two ways: a petition to God to remember…, or a declaration that we offer this sacrifice for…. In the Roman canon the anaphoral intercessions remained relatively restricted in scope. The intercessions in the Alexandrian anaphora of St. Basil and the Antiochene anaphora of the apostles were also relatively brief. Later eucharistic prayers in the West Syrian and Alexandrian traditions, however, were characterized by very lengthy series of intercessions.

The original petition for the church also frequently came to be formulated as a petition for communicants, which might take the form of an invocation of the Holy Spirit upon the communicants that they might enjoy the fruits of communion. Such a petition might also include an invocation of the Holy Spirit upon the gifts as a means for the sanctification of the communicants (as in the anaphora of the *Apostolic Tradition* and the Alexandrian anaphora of St. Basil). Eventually West Syrian anaphoras developed the invocation upon the gifts into a consecratory epiclesis, asking that the Spirit might transform the bread and wine into the body and blood of Christ. This epiclesis is the second form that the expansion of the supplication might take. In the anaphora of St. James, however, the invocation of the Spirit may have developed as an embolism on the Sanctus (like the first epiclesis of the anaphora of St. Mark), which was then separated from the Sanctus when the post-Sanctus, institution narrative, and anamnesis were incorporated into the prayer.

In the Alexandrian and Roman traditions, the supplication also came to include one or more petitions that God would accept the church's offering. It was to such a petition that the institution narrative (coupled with the anamnesis) was appended in the Roman canon, putting this material into the supplication rather than the thanksgiving. In the later Roman tradition, this developed into a specific petition for consecration, which upset the thematic coherence of the eucharistic prayer. The original thematic logic can be seen in the following thematic summary:

Account this offering acceptable...	Quam oblationem
for it is the figure of the body and	
blood of Christ...	
who took the bread and cup and said	Qui pridie
"This is my body, this is my blood...	
Do this in remembrance of me."	
Remembering..., we offer....	Unde et memores
Accept our offering and receive it	Supra quae/Supplices
at the altar on high...	
that the recipients of Christ's body	
and blood may be filled with blessing....	

Here it is really the Supplices that has consecratory force, so that what is offered is the figure of Christ's body and blood, which is then united, when it is received at the altar on high, to Christ's own offering of his body and blood. Giving consecratory force to the Quam oblationem and institution narrative (Qui pridie) destroys the logical coherence of this sequence of petitions in the supplication.

CRAFTING EUCHARISTIC PRAYERS TODAY

The most carefully crafted of the new eucharistic prayers are those which follow the West Syrian pattern. A very common variant in the new eucharistic prayers is the retention of the Western custom of a variable preface. This does not disrupt the West Syrian pattern so long as the post-Sanctus contains at least a brief narrative of God's work of creation and redemption. While few contemporary prayers contain anaphoral intercessions as extensive as those of the classic West Syrian prayers, most retain at least a petition for communicants, often leading into a petition for the coming of God's kingdom.

The Split Epiclesis: A Failed Experiment

The Community of Taizé introduced what has been called the modified West Syrian pattern for contemporary eucharistic prayers. An early eucharistic prayer of this community was a modified form of the Roman canon. The intercessions were removed; an epiclesis based on that of the anaphora of St. Mark linked the Sanctus to a form of the Quam oblationem which included features of both the early and the later Roman form of that petition (describing the gifts as the figures of Christ's sacrifice and asking for their transformation into his body and blood, specifically invoking the Holy Spirit); and the paraphrase of the Supplices included another specific reference to the Holy Spirit. This eucharistic prayer, with a preliminary epiclesis upon the gifts and a second epiclesis upon the communicants, became the model for the new Roman eucharistic prayers and for other eucharistic prayers that treated the words of Christ as consecratory.

This revision of the Roman canon, however, does not really respect the original integrity of the prayer. The original Roman prayer consisted of two petitions that God would accept the church's offering. The first petition, before the institution narrative, offered the bread and wine as figures of Christ's body and blood; the second petition, after the institution narrative and anamnesis, asked God to accept the bread and wine at the heavenly altar, so that those who received them might be partakers of Christ's body and blood. The reworked prayer significantly alters the thematic sequence and integrity of these two petitions. As Nicholas Cabasilas noted centuries ago,[4] the Supplices is the functional equivalent of the consecratory epiclesis of the West Syrian anaphoras: according to the logic of the Roman canon (even in its later form), it is through the sacramental union of the church's offering with the sacrifice which Christ pleads at the heavenly altar that the bread and wine become the body and blood of Christ. By altering the text of the Supplices to ask God to accept the church's prayer (rather than its offering) and by treating the petition as an epiclesis upon the communicants, the author of the Taizé liturgy has drastically changed its function. The modified West Syrian pattern for eucharistic prayers, with a preliminary epiclesis over the gifts and a later epiclesis over the communicants has no real historical precedent, either in the Roman canon or in the Alexandrian tradition (which does have two epicleses, but which treats the *second* epiclesis as consecratory). This pattern is a twentieth-century innovation — and an infelicitous one at that!

Although theologians as early as Ambrose treat the institution narrative as consecratory, it does not serve that function in any of the classical eucharistic prayers except perhaps those of the Mozarabic and Gallican traditions (where it does so by default, since the variable post-Sanctus and post-pridie of these traditions are not thematically stable enough to locate the petition for consecration in them). The theology of consecration by the words of Christ has been *read into* the Roman canon, rather than *derived from* it. It is not really until the eucharistic rites of Luther that we find the institution narrative treated *in liturgical texts* as definitively consecratory. If, nevertheless, contemporary traditions insist on treating this narrative as consecratory, then a double epiclesis such as that of Taizé is justified.

But another problem arises, as we have seen, when eucharistic prayers formulated upon a classical thematic outline treat the institution narrative as consecratory. Most forms of the anamnesis are formulated as an oblation: remembering, we offer. According to the logic of these prayers what is offered in the anamnesis of such prayers can only be the body and blood of Christ. But this is a theology of the eucharistic sacrifice which is doctrinally suspect — a doctrine which Reformation traditions have sought to avoid. For this reason the anamnesis needs to be formulated in such prayers without reference to an oblation of the bread and wine. The anaphora of the apostles provides an alternative here, for it is formulated as a thanksgiving: remembering, we give thanks. Another option is to formulate the anamnesis as an oblation of praise and thanksgiving: remembering, we offer this our sacrifice of praise and thanksgiving. But such formulations can no longer use the bread and wine as the concrete sign of the sacramental union between the church's offering and Christ's sacrifice. On the whole, the West Syrian pattern with its single epiclesis has proved the most fruitful for crafting new eucharistic prayers.

Acclamations

We might think of the Sanctus as the popular acclamation which concludes the (first) thanksgiving. Recent eucharistic prayers have added a memorial acclamation associated with the anamnesis. This acclamation generally comes before the anamnesis. Some critics have argued that it might be more effectively placed after the anamnesis, in order not to break the link between Christ's command in the institution narrative and the church's pledge to fulfil that command in the anamnesis. The Byzantine anaphoras of St. Basil and St. John Chrysostom in fact place a doxological acclamation here. And the acclamation in the prayers of the *United Methodist Hymnal* and the Presbyterian *Book of Common Worship* place memorial acclamations in this position. When placed in this position, a memorial acclamation provides a fitting conclusion to the second thanksgiving, parallel to the Sanctus as the acclamation concluding the first thanksgiving.

The Supplication

The supplication, beginning with the epiclesis, is the third major section of the eucharistic prayer in the West Syrian tradition. In most traditions, it has included a series of intercessions after the epiclesis. If these intercessions are too extensive, they simply duplicate the Prayers of the People in the first part of the eucharistic rite. But in the thematic sequence of the eucharistic prayer, brief petitions are not out of place here. Some contemporary eucharistic prayers also make use of a proper supplication as well as a proper preface. Such a usage makes particular sense at baptisms, marriages, celebrations for the sick, funerals, and on similar occasions. A seasonally varied general supplication, such as we find with North American Methodists and Presbyterians also has much to commend it.

Language for God

An issue which has arisen in the course of recent revisions is that of language for God. Careful theologians as early as Gregory of Nazianzus have noted that gender cannot properly be attributed to God. In the language of prayer, God is addressed in the second person, so that gender-specific pronouns are not an issue. Although the traditional language for the Trinity (Father, Son, and Holy Spirit, or Father, Word, and Spirit), raises problems both of gender attribution and subordination implicit in the metaphors,[5] no satisfactory replacement has yet been found. Recent eucharistic prayers tend to sidestep the problem by addressing the prayer to God (implying the first person, as many traditional collects do), and speaking of Christ and the Holy Spirit. In many ways this is a stop-gap for an issue which is still to be resolved. Recently there has been a tendency to avoid all masculine metaphors for God while cautiously making use of some feminine metaphors. We can see this in the most recent set of eucharistic prayers for the Episcopal Church in the United States, found in *Enriching our Worship*, where all references to God as father have been removed, and a single reference to God as mother is included:

> and yet, as a mother cares for her children,
> you would not forget us.[6]

Surely it would be better to use a richer range of both masculine and feminine metaphors. Perhaps the best way to do this would be to provide a set of prefaces enriched by such metaphors which could be used on occasions "in ordinary time."

Recommendations of the Fifth International Anglican Liturgical Consultation

In 1995 the International Anglican Liturgical Consultation took as its topic the eucharist. Preparatory documents included essays on Eucharistic Theology and Anglican Liturgical Revision; Ecclesiological Reflections on Ministry, Order, and the Eucharist; Towards Renewing the Shape of the Anglican Eucharistic Liturgy; Ritual, Language, and Symbolism in the Eucharist; and Eucharistic Renewal and Liturgical Education. The essay on eucharistic theology has particular relevance to our focus on the eucharistic prayer, its structure and theology. It relies on the research of Thomas Talley and describes as classic a structure for the eucharistic prayer which moves from thanksgiving to supplication and goes on to say:

> It was only with the Scottish and American revisions of the BCP that the classic structure of the prayer was recovered [in the Anglican tradition].
>
> The Western pattern of the eucharistic prayer, with its shift from thanksgiving to supplication after the Sanctus rather than after the anamnesis is, according to Talley, at the root of the theological problems that have developed in the West in relation to the eucharistic rite: the problems of a "moment of consecration"; the thorny issue of memorial, sacrifice, and offering; and the problem of the role of the Spirit and the epiclesis in the eucharistic celebration.[7]

Consequently the essay argues against the use of a split epiclesis:

> The insertion of a "split" epiclesis...[where] the epiclesis before the [institution] narrative is directed toward the elements, and the epiclesis following the narrative is directed toward the communicants...fundamentally obscures the movement from thanksgiving/proclamation to supplication, characteristic of the classic structure of the eucharistic prayer.... If Talley is right, then the invocation of the Spirit ought to follow on from the institution narrative/anamnesis....[8]

All of this is reaffirmed in the working papers of the consultation on eucharistic theology and on the structure of the eucharist. The first of these states:

> We would draw attention to the inter-related character of the tradi-
> tional parts of the eucharistic prayer inclusive of the opening dia-
> logue…, thanksgiving to God for his work in creation, the rehearsal
> of the mighty acts of God in Christ, the anamnesis, the epiclesis of
> the Holy Spirit, petitions, and doxology.

The working paper on the structure of the eucharist notes:

> When the structure links the thanksgiving for creation with the
> Sanctus, the thanksgiving for redemption with the institution narra-
> tive as its proclamatory climax, followed by supplication for the
> work of the Spirit that includes epicletic prayer for the assembly's
> celebration and the church's continuing mission, the prayer has a
> distinctly Trinitarian shape.[9]

This trinitarian shape conforms to the trinitarian character of
eucharistic worship to which the working paper on eucharistic theology gives particular attention.

Other recommendations within this work are worthy of note. In
terms of structure, the placement of the memorial acclamation *after*,
rather than *before*, the anamnesis, is encouraged by the recommenda-
tion that "if responses are used, they should appear between sections of
the prayer and not in the middle of sections."[10] The working paper on
eucharistic theology argues that "the role of the [institution] narrative
emerges more clearly when the congregational acclamation follows the
anamnesis rather than the narrative."[11] Rubrical considerations are also
important in giving visible expression to the structural unity of the
prayer. Two in particular deserve our attention: manual acts during the
institution narrative and posture during the eucharistic prayer. The
working paper on eucharistic theology says of the institution narrative:
"Rather than being a formula for consecration, it is best understood as
the mandate for the performance of the eucharistic action, and the
promise of Christ's presence."[12] The same paper argues that "unity of
the [eucharistic] prayer is emphasized if there are no changes in posture
of either the congregation or presider. Gestures which draw attention to
the institution narrative or any other component may undermine the
essential unity of the prayer."[13]

Issues for the Episcopal Church

The West Syrian structure proved fruitful for the Episcopal Church
in the revision which culminated in the Book of Common Prayer 1979.
The eucharistic prayers which follow that structure— A, B, and D—
have worn well. Several of the issues raised above, however, ought to

be taken into account as the Episcopal Church begins the next revision of its prayer book. First of all, the memorial acclamation should follow the anamnesis of Eucharistic Prayers A and B, as it does in the United Methodist and Presbyterian rites, providing a proper climax to the thanksgiving that begins in the post-Sanctus. Secondly, provision might well be made to include brief intercessory petitions in the supplication of these two prayers (as in the present Prayer D). Eucharistic Prayers B and D already allow for the inclusion of particular saints in the supplication. Similar provisions ought to be made in Eucharistic Prayer A and in new eucharistic prayers. And we should consider proper supplications for feasts, seasons, and pastoral offices in the same way that we provide proper prefaces for these occasions. For an example of such a revision of Eucharistic Prayers A and B, see the Appendix to this Conclusion. The theology of the prayer might be reinforced if the manual acts during the institution narrative were omitted. In terms of structure, the bread and cup are "taken" at the offertory when they are placed on the table; "taking" them again during the institution narrative duplicates this action and gives a misleading impression of the function of the narrative.

Eucharistic Prayer C, felicitous as it is in its language, has worn less well. As an experiment in a different structure for the eucharistic prayer, it "front-loads" both the oblation and the epiclesis into a position before the institution narrative. This is not a structure which the International Consultation recommends and it departs from the tradition of the Episcopal Church in the United States. For the same reason Form 1 (from the Book of Common Prayer) and Form A (from *Enriching our Worship*) for use with An Order for Celebrating the Holy Eucharist stand in need of revision. Eucharistic Prayer C has also been popular because of its use of frequent responses. But the fact that each of these responses is different has the disadvantage of making the congregation book-bound. The revision of this prayer in the Canadian *Book of Alternative Services* corrects both of these problems (conforming the structure to the West Syrian pattern and providing a single response throughout the prayer) and has much to commend it.

Episcopalians are notoriously book-bound worshippers. The provision of different acclamations for each eucharistic prayer only exacerbates this weakness. It would be wiser to provide a single memorial acclamation with a common cue leading into it (as in the present United Methodist rite), or to allow a variety of acclamations, providing each with its own introductory cue (as in the Presbyterian rite).[14] Such a provision would make it easier to use supplementary eucharistic prayers without the necessity of printing out their entire text for worshippers. In a similar way, the cue for the beginning of the Sanctus should be uniform (each of the new prayers in *Enriching our Worship* has a slightly different cue, none of which is the same as that for Eucharistic Prayers A and B).

The issue of the language used to address God is less easily addressed. The eucharistic prayers of *Enriching our Worship* avoid masculine metaphors for God and utilize feminine ones. Surely we should use both for the God who transcends gender. Perhaps the balance might be best addressed by drafting proper prefaces and perhaps proper supplications for ordinary time which make use of feminine metaphors and which might be used with the eucharistic prayers which we now have.

More than two decades of use have revealed ways in which the Book of Common Prayer 1979 might be enriched and improved. But the Episcopal Church at this time might be wise to continue to issue supplementary resources (including schedules of permitted revisions of the present eucharistic prayers and new eucharistic prayers) rather than to undertake the production of a new Book of Common Prayer in the immediate future.

Another issue worth considering is our evaluation of the eucharistic prayers of other churches with whom we are in ecumenical dialogue. From the perspective of historical theology, the minimum requirement for a eucharistic prayer established by a proper exegesis of the accounts of the last supper is that such a prayer offer thanks to God and that it be the means of the remembrance of Christ. The contemporary prayers of most traditions certainly meet this requirement.

A favorable response to the Called to Common Mission has brought us into full communion with the Evangelical Lutheran Church. It seems appropriate, therefore, to authorize for use by Episcopal clergy, when the pastoral occasion warrants, the eucharistic rite of the *Lutheran Book of Worship*, with the provision that a full eucharistic prayer be used. While we should respect the older tradition, rooted in Luther's writings, that the church consecrates by proclaiming the eucharistic gospel rather than by offering a eucharistic prayer, it is surely reasonable to bind our clergy, when celebrating according to the *Lutheran Book of Worship*, to the use of a full eucharistic prayer.

In ecumenical contexts, it would also seem appropriate to authorize Episcopal clergy to concelebrate the eucharist using the rites in the *United Methodist Hymnal*, the United Church of Christ's *Book of Worship*, and (when the institution narrative is included) the Presbyterian *Book of Common Worship*. In each of these cases, the eucharistic prayers conform to the Episcopal Church's understanding of how the church gives thanks at the eucharist. The text of the eucharistic prayer in the COCU rite presents no problems from a theological perspective, but it would seem preferable to use on occasions of concelebration a eucharistic prayer that is actually in regular use in one of the churches. The Lima liturgy of the World Council of Churches has also been authorized in the past for use in concelebrations, but it shares the defects of the modified West Syrian structure first proposed by the Taizé community.

At the beginning of the third millennium, let us rejoice in the good and joyful offering which is becoming once again the principal service of the Christian church as it celebrates the Lord's Day.

NOTES

[1] W. Jardine Grisbrooke, s.v. "Anaphora," in J. G. Davies, ed., *The New Westminster Dictionary of Liturgy and Worship* (Philadelphia: Westminster Press, 1986), pages 13-21, here 14-15.

[2] Ibid., page 15.

[3] For an analysis of the diptychs, see Robert Taft, *A History of the Liturgy of St. John Chrysostom. Volume IV: The Diptychs.*

[4] Nicholas Cabasilas, *A Commentary on the Divine Liturgy* (London: SPCK, 1960), § 30, pages 76-79.

[5] See the discussion in Brian Wren, *What Language Shall I Borrow? God-Talk in Worship: A Male Response to Feminist Theology* (New York: Crossroad, 1989), chapter 8.

[6] Eucharistic Prayer 2, in *Enriching our Worship: Supplemental Liturgical Materials Prepared by the Standing Liturgical Commission* (New York: Church Publishing, 1998), page 60.

[7] David R. Holeton, ed., *Our Thanks and Praise: The Eucharist in Anglicanism Today. Papers from the Fifth International Anglican Liturgical Consultation* (Toronto: Anglican Book Centre, 1998), page 39.

[8] Ibid., page 48.

[9] Ibid., page 287. The printed text reads "following by," surely a misprint for "followed by."

[10] Ibid., page 288 (working paper on the structure of the eucharist).

[11] Ibid., page 289.

[12] Ibid., page 269.

[13] Ibid., page 288.

[14] It might be well to use only the acclamations found at present in Eucharistic Prayers A and B. The other two acclamations in common use (one of which is attached to Eucharistic Prayer 3 in *Enriching our Worship*) are addressed to Christ and therefore fit awkwardly into prayers addressed to the first person of the Trinity.

APPENDIX
A Revision of Eucharistic Prayers A and B

EUCHARISTIC PRAYER A

The following text comes immediately after the narrative of the institution.

We celebrate the memorial of our redemption, O Father, in this sacrifice of praise and thanksgiving. Recalling his death, resurrection, and ascension, we offer you these gifts.

Great is the mystery of our faith:

Celebrant and People

Christ has died,
Christ is risen,
Christ will come again.

The Celebrant continues

Sanctify these gifts by your Holy Spirit to be for your people the Body and Blood of your Son, the holy food and drink of new and everlasting life. Sanctify us also that we may faithfully receive this holy Sacrament, and serve you in unity, constancy, and peace.

[*Particular intercessions may be included here, each petition beginning,* Remember....]

[*Proper supplications may follow, such as this supplication for Holy Week.*:

Lead us, O God, in the way of Christ. Give us courage to take up our cross, and, in full reliance upon your grace, to follow him.]

And at the last day bring us with [_____ and] all your saints into the joy of your eternal kingdom.

All this we ask....

EUCHARISTIC PRAYER B

The following text comes immediately after the narrative of the institution.

Remembering his death, resurrection, and ascension, O Lord of all, we offer our sacrifice of praise and thanksgiving to you, presenting to you, from your creation, this bread and this wine.

According to Christ's commandment:

Celebrant and People

We remember his death,
We proclaim his resurrection,
We await his coming in glory.

The Celebrant continues

We pray you, gracious God, to send your Holy Spirit upon these gifts that they may be the Sacrament of the Body of Christ and his Blood of the new Covenant. Unite us to your Son in his sacrifice, that we may be acceptable through him, being sanctified by the Holy Spirit.

[*Particular intercessions may be included here, each petition beginning,* Remember....]

[*Proper supplications may follow, such as this supplication for Holy Week*:

Lead us, O God, in the way of Christ. Give us courage to take up our cross, and, in full reliance upon your grace, to follow him.]

In the fullness of time, reconcile all things in Christ, and bring us to that heavenly country....